T0366180

MUSINGS OF A FIRST CHINESE DAUGHTER

A MEMOIR

JENNIFER LEE ROBERTSON

PARTRIDGE

A Penguin Random House Company

To order additional copies of this book, contact
Toll Free 800 101 2657 (Singapore)
Toll Free 1 800 81 7340 (Malaysia)
orders.singapore@partridgepublishing.com

www.partridgepublishing.com/singapore

CONTENTS

DEDICATION PAGE

Li-Yünyen

Mary Ying-Chen

In loving memory of my father and mother.

"And if I go, while you're still here . . .
Know that I live on, vibrating to a different
measure—
You will not see me, so you must have faith . . .
Just whisper my name in your heart . . . I will be
there."

* C. Jones, *Through A Glass Darkly—A Journey of Love and Grief with my Father*, ABCBooks, pub 2009.

ACKNOWLEDGEMENTS

I n writing this book, I have been deeply indebted to the following people whose help have been instrumental in the publication of this book. I wish to thank the following; (names are in alphabetical order):

Dr. Rod Bucknell for editing and invaluable contribution of Chinese characters and translations; Vanessa de Voss, for her time, editing and comment; Leslie James, for assistance with suggestion of possible sources of research material on Sago Lane; Anne-Marie Marias, in encouragement and suggestion of possible publishers; Caroline Pickering, in assistance with comment and editing; Raymond Robertson, for necessary contribution and preparation of all photos/images, and in particular, essential advice and management of the computer.

PREFACE

MUSINGS OF A FIRST CHINESE DAUGHTER

This is a memoir of my parents, with the focus on my father, whose resilience and mischievous sense of humour kept him afloat throughout his difficult life, but which could not save him from a tragic end. My father passed away in 1960 and with him, I see the passing away of traditional Chinese culture, idealism and romance, which have shaped the Chinese mind for centuries. In this fast-changing world, Modern China is racing ahead to attain the status of economic superpower, and the gap between the Old and the New China seems to be widening by the day. In the Confucian hierarchy, the business class was at the bottom rung of the social ladder—Deng Xiaoping's hymn "To make money is glorious" would not be sounding too glorious to the Celestial Empire of the past. My parents' China, burnt and burnished by series of tumultuous upheavals, bloodshed and humiliations, would, seem to me, to colour China's present stance on the world stage.

This memoir is not written in story format. It is more a literary pastiche—a montage of my world in Australia juxtaposed against the rich philosophical and cultural heritage that my traditional Chinese parents represented.

The writing, therefore, is heavily laced with the woof and warp of the ornate tapestry of the vibrant culture of a by-gone Chinese world. The chapters are not in strict chronological order: there is no story line; the hero and heroine are my parents, whose resilience and courage showcase the struggle of Everyman. I believe that the recognition and admiration of a person need not be based on surmounting dangers of epic proportions.

The book acknowledges that change is inevitable; but what is humane in the world must not be and cannot be traded off—especially in the face of the pervasive power of the digital and cyber-world that can desensitise some of its impressionable devotees. In paying a tribute to my parents and the past generations, the book celebrates the fact that this "humaneness", this innate goodness in mankind, is very much alive here today—in the raw courage of those who answer the call to protect lives, in our iconic Diggers, in our sense of fair play and mateship, in our fleet of volunteers, in the wonderful men and women of the SES (State Emergency Service) in times of tribulations and sorrows; in the struggle of the ordinary mum and dad, manifesting their unconditional love of their children . . . The Honour list is long indeed.

Father had a profound influence on my life, on the little girl in the book. Whenever there appears an observation on current issues, my father's voice seems to echo through the mist of my treasured past. His persona in my dream is still very much alive today.

I hope that by drawing upon history, Confucian idealism, Daoist and Buddhist influence on China, I can convey a glimpse of what shaped the thinking and outlook of my traditional parents—the Chinese Mind.

Jennifer Lee Robertson.

CHAPTER 1

THAT WAS THEN, THIS IS NOW

A dream! A dream! I had a dream! An extraordinary dream where I seemed to be with my father gazing out of a window at the bustling life below us. We seemed to be in some kind of virtual city—Brisbane, and yet unlike Brisbane. The silent bustling city below was a familiar city scene, could be anywhere in Australia except for its weird silence. Father seemed to be prancing around in great excitement and astonishment. He was fascinated by the many wired young people. The scene was a busy place of wired young people with ipads and laptops wrapped up in their own private worlds. What excited father most was the sight of skyscrapers and fast cars; and of course, his exclamation of "Bridge to Heaven! Look! Look!" was meant for the sky train and the traffic on the overhead pass. He simply could not take his eyes off the caterpillar sinuous movement of the road train.

This surreal silent world allowed me no response to father's cascade of rhetorical questions and comments which frothed and frizzled about me, swamping me in an eddy of breathlessness as well. The occasion transported me to that moment in 1955 when the entire family had rushed to the front door drawn by father's excited shouts and gesticulation to what was on the street—"A shoe! A shoe! A mobile shoe!" It was a Volkswagen which was cruising to a stop in front of our house. (It did look like a popular brand of sports shoes on sale then.) It was no surprise to me, then, to witness father's excited wonder at what he saw in the dream.

We have certainly come a long way in just under a decade from that day! My father passed away in 1960. CHANGE, that magic weapon is invincible—nothing can ever remain static—life has changed, attitudes and values have changed, my strict traditional Chinese upbringing has change—it has been adulterated . . . cultures have become multi-faceted . . .

Father, with his traditional upbringing, fresh from the humiliation of the Opium Wars of the 1840s (responsible for the nadir of Chinese history) would never recognize the China of today. My father's traditional Chinese world with its rich cultural heritage is gone—my meandering through the fog of my parents' life and my upbringing is an attempt to recapture that past and to take a peek into what constituted the Chinese Mind of the traditional past—my father's world would be a fairly safe place to start. Father had enriched our lives with tales and myths of a colorful past that perhaps, no young technological nerd of today would care to explore. His outlook and attitude towards life was shaped by China's history of glory and shame.

The cultural heritage of my father's world will soon fade into a forgotten limbo. I am grateful to him for helping me to enjoy the twilight glow of China's visionary golden age in my childhood. The current of changes today is too rapid and breath-taking. My world of today is fast evolving into another 'Brave New World'; and as I journey along, the snapshots of my childhood embodied in the rich brocade of father's China will be interlaced with today's pulsating changes of a very diverse scenario.

Today's China is an entirely different universe—China, the wounded dragon of my parents' day has recovered to snarl for the title of world power. In the mad chase after the almighty dollar, my parents' China of *The Romance of the Three Kingdoms* and *The Dreams of the Red Chamber* has given way to crass greed and ruthlessness. China seems to be in a great hurry; there is no time for a backward glance. Those left in the remote areas, caught in a time warp are confused. It is fascinating to note that today's digital China with a population of over 1.4 billion (one and a half times that of Europe, Russia and Turkey combined) has yet to come into her own with regard to scientific and technical terms. 火車 huoche, the word for 'train' literally mean 'fire car' — reminiscent of trains of yesteryear, fuelled by wood fire. Yet, China is responsible for showcasing the fastest high-speed train in the planet with the speed of about 400 kilometre per hour, (a project in 2013.) Aeroplane 飛機— feiji is still known as 'flying machine'. The characters for road, 馬車路 ma che lu retain the ancient terminology of 'horse-cart track'. To say "on horseback I come" 馬上來 ma shang lai, means "I'm coming immediately."

Father's traditional Chinese mind values one's unique ethnicity. He upheld the view that one's cultural heritage is the intellectual mine of the valuable, the elegant, the brilliant, the beautiful and the rigorous harvest of generations. China's history, bathed in blood and intrigues, has also brought to the surface Man's resilience and supreme capacity for love and sacrifice. Father's world expected decorum in behavior and modesty in attire. The moral compass was regulated by the concept of Responsibility and Respect—self-respect and respect for others at all times. Yes, the dream was a very alien world to father.

Father seemed to be particularly amazed by the sloppy appearance of many people and he was most astonished by the amount of flesh exposed by women of all ages, shapes and sizes. This was to be expected because women in traditional China were expected to be well covered, especially in public. He seemed to be genuinely perplexed that some people could be so careless as not to plan well enough in cutting their materials to size. Father helpfully conceded that exposing one's belly was indeed a good way to cool oneself, but then, surely not for a lady? He seemed particularly concerned that some of the ladies' pants were in danger of slipping off. Part of the buttock was clearly having a peek at the world and he did wonder if it was in need of cooling as well. It was all too strange to him. In short, father seemed not only transfixed with avid curiosity and wonderment; at times, he seemed positively aghast.

Was he in fantasyland, he wondered. Buddhism teaches that the world itself is in a state of flux and life is an illusion. Illusion! Illusion! All is illusion! Father's tremulous voice of wonderment steadily dissolved with him into the dark void . . .

Changes? Of course our world today has changed beyond father's comprehension. Humanity has always been tossed about in the current of fantastic changes and metamorphoses which seem to be accelerating at an alarming speed and I myself find it hard to comprehend. At the ebbing of the tidal wave I, too, will soon be a blinking dinosaur. My parents would find it difficult to foresee that within their life span, high-speed travel would become a reality and that the Kitty Hawk of the Wright brothers in 1903 would magically morph into an air-bus.

This writing is a humble attempt to salute the older generations whose resilience in the face of challenges has equipped them to keep up with the pace of Change It seems to me that it has always been the lot of preceding generations to take the back seat in the inevitability of change which wears the label of "modernization" and "progress". Each wave of change would rock the social framework of the day because new values and attitudes would undermine traditional mores and beliefs. The older generations have not only to contend with the generation gap between themselves and their offspring, but those who have chosen to migrate have to face the additional dilemma of culture clash and the need to assimilate. I consider myself very lucky to be living in Australia. Australia with its smorgasbord of multicultural delights can be exciting, challenging and painful, depending on which side of the fence one is on. There are different tempos to the drumbeat—just as the cavalier attitude to sex is the IN thing to some, we have others who still cling fastidiously to "Honour-killing" if an unfortunate female in the family chooses to marry someone of her choice.

In my childhood days, our concept of a burglar was coloured by the tongue-in-cheek cartoon of a masked man with a ladder about to break into a building for a mere pittance by our current standard. Today, we have the cool sleuth who can cream off millions of dollars from the comfort of his computer swivel chair. Our smart burglar (no mask needed) can, with a tap on the computer keys hold the world to ransom. Fascinating!

We have much to be grateful for in our technological advancement and progress especially in the field of medical science. Life has been made so much easier and enjoyable; but somehow, spiritually and intellectually, there seems to be an uncomfortable vacuum. When I thought that the signposts to a more caring and responsible society with decent expectations and values seemed to be rather obscure, when lo and behold! in our fair land, in marched the thousands of volunteers when tragedy struck—natural disasters like floods and bush fires bring out the best in people. The SES, the State Emergency Service people and volunteers deserve special honour—what higher selfless sacrifice can one give than these people do as they give their best to others at all times! Father would be proud of this and he would happily remind me that Mencius, (372-289 BC), one of Confucius' most brilliant students, believed that mankind is inherently good.

Maybe, people like my naïve and trusting parents of the last century seemed less lost; their world-view had been moulded by a starkly different culture—the traditional Chinese culture had stringent rules and boundaries regarding what were expected of a responsible, moral individual. There are some valuable tenets in the teachings which cannot become out-of-date; they should contribute to a more orderly and "moral" world. This by no means suggests that I advocate a return to the past. Our democratic world view has brought about wonderful changes—China has galloped ahead—for a start, women in urban China can celebrate their new status of equality with their menfolk.

Poor treatment of women seems to be ingrained in many cultures. Father was pleased that China had progressively banned the practice of what was unfair and caused unnecessary suffering to society. This includes the practice of foot-binding, "the guilty until proved innocent" principle in law, honour killing, and inequality of the sexes. Changes will be slow in some cases, especially mutilation of the sexual organs or body, which stemmed from cultural expectations of the past. In some rural provinces of developing countries, child brides are common and the practice of "sati", the sacrificial burning of widows, though very rare, is still known to be in practice even though the British had attempted to ban it when it colonized India. Why a widow who had faced the tragedy of the loss of her husband, the main breadwinner of the family, should have to face a horrible death just to prove her chastity is a question that never seemed to be asked. The widower, on the other hand, was free to look forward to getting a sweet, young thing for his nuptial bed.

It is accepted that a man is free to "sow his wild oats" but this privilege is not interchangeable—society still frowns on a woman who hops from bed to bed. Marriage endows a woman with some respectability; the term "spinster" lacks the charming resonance of a "bachelor".

What a confusing world! In my next reincarnation, I think I'd vote to come to this earth as a prized stud bull to service hundreds of cows! I don't have to work for a living—my service would be every cow's desire before they end up as steak on your table. I'd be admired and desired and die a natural death of old age. No steak from this macho stud!

Status in the traditional Chinese family was codified in the famous "three bonds", as emphasized by Confucius and the learned scholars: the bond of loyalty on the part of subject to ruler—the crime of treachery to one's emperor or country would merit the worst of punishment—death by hanging was not sufficient, he had to be quartered; bond of filial obedience on the part of son to father; and, of chastity on the part of wives, but not of husbands. The lord and master of the family would get off scot-free of course; he could marry as many women as he could afford to keep them.

Confucius' teaching emphasized the importance of filial piety which is very much tied to the matter of ancestor worship. I had heard many stories on this subject when bouncing on my father's knees at the age of 4 or 5, but was too young to absorb all of them. One which seemed to be carved in my young mind was the story of an important official of the court who had to return home each night to his aged father. Unfortunately, there had been a colossal flood which swept away everything in its path. It was a dark night and though it was a losing death-defying swim across to his abode, the official did struggle through to carry his aged father on his shoulders, only to be drowned. In the context of today, such a feat would be seen as foolish—but then, so important was the code of filial piety that perishing in the attempt would be more preferable to a life of shame.

Women of today have not only made inroads into male domain, some have become very efficient and respected heads of states. It is interesting to note that though downtrodden throughout the ages, yet women throughout history have rocked the world—Helen of Troy whose beauty "launched a thousand ships"; the "virgin" Queen of England, Elizabeth the First, was able to maintain control against great odds in one of England's golden eras; and let us not forget Cleopatra, whose beauty transformed empires. One of the most powerful women in Chinese history was the notorious Empress Dowager of the late Qing Dynasty. She was instrumental in the loss of millions of lives and was responsible for the carving up of China by the rapacious power-hungry colonists in the nineteenth century. Even little Japan had a big chunk of the pie.

Apart from the rapacious Empress Dowager, there had been many other women in China who made a fair contribution towards traditional Chinese history. Many a poem and operas were based on their silent suffering and their brush with fame which changed the course of history. One of the famous episodes in history, which contributed to the collapse of an empire, was that of Yang Guifei of the famous Tang Dynasty (618-906AD)

The poem quoted below is based on Bai Juyi's poem *"The Song of Everlasting Sorrow."*

The infinitely sad theme is the ill-fated romance between the ageing Emperor Xuanzong of the Tang Dynasty and his favourite concubine Yang Guifei. The Emperor was over 60 years old when they met. He already had 30 sons and 29 daughters. She was in her late teens.

What I remember from my father's story and from history that I gathered later on, was that Yang Guifei had been sent by her family to seduce the Tang Emperor with the aim of weakening the empire to facilitate a take-over by An Lu Shan's rebel groups. This she did very, very well indeed, because the emperor became so infatuated with her that he let the affairs of state go to ruin. The rebel groups were soon overrunning the country. Wrote Bai Juyi:

". . . And thence, the emperor ceased to hold morning court
For sunrise was untimely, the night was too short."

What made this an epic opera was that the poor emperor was genuinely in love with her—she was his life and they had a very happy love-life for twelve years before he lost her. He was totally besotted by her:

> "She turned her head, a single smile,
>   A hundred charms were born—
> The beauties of Six Palaces
>   Of all their looks were shorn."

She flashed him a fleeting coy smile, hid her face behind her fan and he was lost forever!

The mandarins at court decided that the only way to save the empire was to have her killed at the earliest opportunity. So on this day, while the royal couple were fleeing from the capital ahead of the tidal wave of rebels, the mandarins decided that no time must be lost—the emperor had to face the ultimatum—the empire or the femme fatale.

They stopped the royal chariot and performed the grisly task.

> The soldiers of the army stopped,
>   They would no further ride,
> Till sinking at their horses' hooves,
>   The moth-eyed beauty died.
> Kingfisher plumes and golden pins
>   And jade-carved diadem,
> Her combs inlaid with flowers lay strewn
>   And no man gathered them.
> The Emperor could not spare her life;
>   He turned his head around.
> When he turned back, his tears of grief
>   Spattered the blood-soaked ground.
> A shrill and bitter wind sprang up
>   The yellow dust swirled round. [*1]

Her tragic death had so galvanised everybody that not even the half-starved soldiers cared to pick up any of her fallen treasures.

The emperor could not save her life—

This has a special resonance with traditional China. The Emperor of China was the Celestial Son of Heaven to whom the entire world owed sacred obeisance. However! The Son of Heaven would lose his Mandate to rule if he had not adhered to his Royal Duty. In extreme circumstances, natural disasters, which wrought havoc on his kingdom, could be construed as his loss of Mandate. The tragic Tang Emperor here had lost his right to rule. He was therefore totally powerless—he had to watch her die . . .

What could be more desolate than—"the yellow dust swirled round the spattered blood-soaked ground."

After the rebellion was over, he was able to return to the desolate palace where, "the steps were heaped with crimson leaves. That no one swept away."

He had lost all care of everything—the loneliness and desolation of his life could be summed up in the phrase . . . 'crimson leaves'—dying leaves.

He abdicated in favour of his son.

CHAPTER 2

"ANOINTED WITH FRAGRANCE, SHE TAKES LOTUS STEPS."

The Western world has its femme fatales in the persons of Helen of Troy and Cleopatra. Traditional China has her Yang Guifei whose sexual charm brought about the demise of the Tang Emperor (618-916 AD).

Not so grandiose, however, but as heart-wrenching were the lives of millions of unfortunate women especially those born into poor families in traditional China. The aim of every family was to get their daughters married off—women had no lives of their own; they had to depend on a husband for a living. The boy-meets-girl scenario that leads to their "falling in love" which we enjoy today was an unknown privilege. It was the practice to have arranged marriages by match-makers. Unfortunately, these people could be quite ruthless, since all they were interested in was to be paid for a successful marriage arrangement. They had the convenient advantage to know that in nearly all cases, the potential brides and grooms and their respective families had no idea of each other's existence. The brides and grooms would only see each other for the first time on their wedding night. Some of these match-makers could be sufficiently unscrupulous as to take advantage of the fact that some starving families often considered their young daughters as a valuable commodity. In effect these child brides (some often as young as twelve years old) were often sold for a mere pittance—as insignificant as a sack of rice. Stories have been told of parents selling their children to pay off a debt, or an opium-addicted father selling his daughter to feed his craving. Parents in these dire straits would not think twice if their child was sold to a decrepit invalid or a man old enough to be their child's grandfather.

In many parts of the world, only male children were worth given an education for obvious reasons. This was especially so in traditional China—a son in a Chinese family is of paramount importance not only because he is expected to be the chief breadwinner in the family, but he is valued for the fact that he is the one to perpetuate the family line. A traditional Chinese woman was expected to adopt the husband's surname as a replacement of her family name. This has earned her the label of being the inferior sex. If a traditional country like Japan is willing to legislate that a female could be considered heir to the Chrysanthemum Throne, this can be seen as a hopeful start to promote equality between the sexes. Our current popular practice of married women adopting a hyphenated surname—their husbands' and their family names bodes well for our society today.

We all recognize that the urge to enhance one's sex appeal is a natural instinct. In today's world, if a girl chooses to starve herself to look like a stick-insect just because beauty is seen to be equated with slimness, she would regard her choice as her democratic right. However! There was no such right in the traditional Chinese world; it was a case of one sexual group enforcing a form of torture—foot-binding on the female sex just for their own sexual gratification. This aberration of Human Right which should have died a natural death ages ago, failed to be totally banned till 1920.

There were a couple of myths about when and why foot-binding became a national fetish. One legend attributed its origin to the Shang Dynasty (1700-1027 BC) that one of the daughters of the Emperor was born with a club foot and he decreed that the Court ladies should have their feet bound to reduce their size. A more popular version pointed to the Emperor of the Tang Dynasty (618-906AD). It appeared that he had been most impressed by one of his concubines who had bound her feet to suggest the shape of a crescent moon in her performance of a "lotus dance". This poem was written by an early Song statesman-poet Su Shi (1036-1101):

> "Anointed with fragrance, she takes lotus steps:
> Though often sad, she steps with swift lightness;
> She dances like the wind, leaving no physical trace:
> . . . ."

That women had their feet bound to discourage their running away from home was a flimsy excuse. The main reason was to satisfy the male fetish—sexual arousal from seeing a woman swaying her hips! The feet were bound to deliberately deform them into the shape of a ball so the woman had no choice but to sway on the deformed ball-shape feet. The aim was to reduce the foot to a 4-inch-long "golden lily"; and there were special slippers to cover the misshapened feet at bedtime. A woman's bound feet were supposed to bring as much erotic arousal as her breasts.

Originally, foot-binding was only restricted to the elite class and rich families. It soon became accepted that women with bound feet would come from the upper classes. Unfortunately, vanity had spread this practice to the lower classes as well because of the attached social prestige. Peasant families who were mainly farmers from South China had been held in derision—they were labeled 'Big Feet' and I still remember the unfair ridicule this term had been flung at the Hakka dialect group.

Foot-binding had to be started young—as young as 5 to 8 years old and the unutterable suffering of this poor child would last until the feet stopped growing when she was 13-15 years old. During this critical period, her feet were always bound up with strips of binding cloth, (about ten feet long) day and night, with no let-up in order to maintain the pressure of crushing the growing bones. To make the feet thinner under the constant pressure, the four minor toes on each foot were pushed down around and under the balls of the feet. Under this intense constant pressure, the arches of the feet would have been gradually broken and bowed upward so only the back edge of the heels would support the girl's weight. As the arch was gradually broken the heels and balls of the feet were gradually moved from horizontal to perpendicular, facing each other, so that an object like a silver coin could be inserted in the narrow space between them.

*1 The Four-inch Lily

The girl would never be able to run or walk in the normal fashion again. Even standing would be uncomfortable. After the feet had stopped growing in mid-teen, the pain would have been abated but the binding cloths remained, partly because the feet needed support and partly because they would be ugly to look at. The child's only solace would be the experienced mum who had carried the same cross. Mum would teach her the art of not blocking the circulation lest it produced gangrene and pus; mum would advise her to keep the bent-under toenails short to prevent puncturing the skin; mum would teach her to change the bindings daily to keep the pressure even; of washing to reduce stench and how to massage the legs to reduce pain. Mum would help to choose the right cute little shoes to advertise her achievement of being an enticing commodity on the marriage market. Marriage match-makers had always stressed the importance of tiny foot size.

*2 shoe of a well-to-do lady.

Woe betides the poor bound-foot servant who had to be in constant attendance on her employer. Her hope would lie in her mistress, whose feet had also been tortured to shape like hers, and who might at least release her from unnecessary standing while she relished her shark's fins soup and inhaled her fragrant tea. Missionaries in the 1800's had maintained that about 10% of the girls who underwent foot-binding did not survive the ordeal.

My first encounter with a bound foot woman was in the person of Mrs. Sim who happened to be our co-tenant. It was in the 1940s that some women chose to unbind their feet. Mrs. Sim was one of these but she still tottered painfully on the pathetic little deformities. She said that the pain of taking off the cloth bindings had been excruciating but it was preferable to the daily torture of having to unbind to clean her feet each night. The painful ordeal of this nocturnal cleansing ritual was always unbearable because of an overpowering stench as well.

Mrs. Sim and her four children had to huddle in a tiny bedroom for that was what they could afford. She had only one bed in her tiny bedroom, so some members of the family had to sleep on the floor outside their bedroom. The eldest was a boy of about 20; his name was Stinking Pig. Chinese value their male offspring so much that they just cannot afford to lose any of them to the jealous gods who may take them away. So to protect their sons, the poor boys would be given derogatory "pet" names. These were generally named after some animals and as a form of double precaution, the anxious parents would add the choicest degrading appellations to the names. One would, therefore, come across precious sons bearing names such as Dirty Skunk, Filthy Dog or even Lousy Devil for the rest of their lives. Of course, officially, they would have their proper family names on record.

Girls, on the other hand, were dispensable. Parents would fearlessly flaunt their names in style with popular names such as Precious Jade, Rare Diamond, Treasured Gold other than more neutral feminine names such as Delicate Peony, Fragrant Rose, Wispy Cloud etc. Mrs. Sim's two daughters were named Precious Treasure and Precious Pearl. It would be common courtesy for one to address someone's daughter as "Thousand Gold" if her name was not known.

I don't recall why Precious Treasure, the eldest daughter of about 17 had the privilege of attending a Chinese School while the 2nd, daughter, Precious Pearl, age 14, had to help in the family "business" which was an ice and fruit cart at a busy junction of 2 busy streets opposite a bus terminus. The stall featured sweet and cake delicacies, ices, jellies and fruits kept cool sitting on ice blocks. Mrs Sim was the boss-manager who decided who had to be on duty at the stall.

It was always high drama came Precious Pearl's turn to be on duty—she would scream and yell at the top of her voice, tear her hair and stomp about in hysterical anger— in short, her tearful howls of anger could be heard a block away. This explosive hysteria always erupted because Stinking Pig would go off duty without replenishing fresh fruits. Precious Pearl would lose her precious voice over the fact that she had to prepare fresh fruits and she specially disliked peeling and cutting spikey pineapples. I used to watch her in fascination when she was in one of her usual tantrums. Her distorted face would reduce her eyes to two thin slits and the face became one large cavern of a mouth. Her angry howls and hair-tearing could rival any Greek Tragic Drama! Then, just as sudden as the heart-wrenching opera had erupted, that howl would be checked in mid crescendo—poor mum had stepped in to take over the offending chore.

I suspected that poor Precious Pearl had to perform a man's job outdoor—sitting at a street stall because Mrs Sim needed someone on roster. The older sister, however, being nearer to "marriage age" had to be cloistered indoors as proper young ladies should. She was the one who had the privilege of swanning past her mother's fruit stall on her way home from school and without any seeming acknowledgement of the presence of the stall, she would, with graceful dignity, surreptitiously indicate which iced delicacy she had wished to partake of at home. The waiter, youngest son, Little Flea, would promptly deliver the delicacy to big sister.

Precious Treasure's ice-cold demeanor was only a public veneer—shapely, fair with almond-shaped eyes, Precious Treasure would often beguile herself in front of the mirror with various samples of dimpled smiles. Precious Treasure, her family's pride and joy would be docile and ever ready to please only one person in the world—her useless father. We hardly ever saw the father at home—in fact, home was a place he dropped in occasionally when he needed money. Just as darkness descends upon a sun-drenched field when an errant cloud drifts across the sun, Mr. Sim's presence had the magic of casting a pall of silence and tension on the family. He was a bowed, little man of about five feet four with a hunched back. He had shifty down-cast eyes and his thin, mottled dark grey lips were always tightly pursed. I had never heard him utter a single word. All we knew was that he was an opium-addict who never seemed to be home. He acknowledged Precious Treasure's winning smiles with a grunt which seemed to be the family's only reward from him. Mrs. Sim who slogged day and night over the iced-fruit cart had to hand over whatever amount of money he needed without receiving any form of appreciation from this odious specimen who would sidle into the family room silently and just as silently would evaporate into his chosen opium den, somewhere.

This unsavory character was a living example of what authority a man of the house could wield—even when he was a burden to a wife with bound feet, whose life rotated around that little cart which needed to be painfully pushed onto site at first light and be cleaned and restocked late at night. Mrs. Sim and her family reflected a typical traditional family where the wife counted for nothing— the man, even the ilkes of this slimy Sim, who was a millstone round one's neck could still command the obedience and respect of his family. Women like Mrs. Sim had to undergo severe torture to have their feet bound to gratify a man's selfish appetite. Only match-making would land someone with a creature like her husband. Perhaps Mrs. Sim was a lucky woman after all! That he had an addiction in opium and he could be so easily bought off with handouts! Mr. Sim was one of the millions of Chinese who fell victim to the Opium Wars that began in 1840, and which failed to prevent the dumping of opium into China by the British. Opium-smoking was only finally eradicated by the Communist Government when it came into power in 1949.

If getting a husband through match-making was a life-shattering gamble, the poor bride had to hold her breath to face the other big nightmare—the demon of a mother-in-law. Stories had been richly spiced about their tyrannical oppression of daughters-in-law from whom they exacted absolute obedience and servitude. Young brides should really take note of a Han mother's advice to her daughter:

"When you go to your husband's house, do not behave well, for whatever you do well will be wrong in any case."[*3]

Divorce was a social stigma. A wife was expected to remain faithful to her husband for life. The husband, on the other hand, enjoyed the privilege of having concubines, as many as he liked. Wives and concubines who attempted to conspire against the husband would be treated to the most severe of punishment—death by slow slicing. There was a story about a warlord, a Zhang Zongchong, who had about forty concubines from different nationalities. He was known as the "General Three Don't Knows". He had no idea how many concubines he owned, how much money he had, and no clue at all how many men were under his command.

Since a divorce was not an option for an unhappy wife, the best insurance for her was to produce a son. This could be a passport for gaining some privileges. Not all unhappy wives however, were like my stoic Mrs. Sim who allowed her useless husband to exploit her and her family for life. In the final analysis, the best weapon to counter a heartless husband and a domineering mother-in-law lies in the wife's personality and strength of character.

A foreigner in the nineteenth century wrote:

"If she is able, at a moment's notice to raise a tornado and keep it blowing at the rate of 100 miles an hour, then the most termagant of mothers-in-law hesitates to attack one who has no fear of men or demons. Alternately, she could refuse to speak at all under all provocation preserving a powerful and radiating silence".[*4]

There could be another alternative—the wife could threaten suicide upon the family. The mother-in-law would then be obliged to be part of the party of mourners to follow her coffin. This would not only attract public ridicule of her being an oppressive bully, but it could also possibly attract court action by the family of the deceased.

It is unclear how far back in Chinese History that the female sex had been regarded as less superior to the male. Any derogatory term such as "evil", "avarice" . . . would have the "woman" character as part of its component. Very early in history, sensuality and sexual appetite appear to be more firmly associated with women than with men. Confucius in the sixth century had been known to utter this contemptuous remark: "We should not be too familiar with the lower orders or with women."

Sima Qian, a great historian in the period of the Han dynasty had a story about a famous Han General, Sun Wu who had been requested by the Emperor to demonstrate his military theory by training 180 women. Sun Wu divided the women into two companies with the Emperor's favourite concubines as leaders. He explained the rules of the drill to the ladies and decided to give the order after he had been assured that they had fully understood him. Then the drum rolled and the order 'Turn right!' was given. The ladies burst out laughing. When this happened a second time, Sun Wu was prepared to execute the Company Leaders. The emperor watching from the Imperial stand sent two messengers saying: "I can see you are an able general. But without these two concubines, my food would lose all flavors."

Sun Wu had them executed.*5

Concubines or wives, men cannot do without them. "May you have a hundred sons and a thousand grandchildren" still exists as a popular greeting to the newlyweds. Men's vanity has led them to eat anything that could promote their virility. The tills in Chinese herbal shops are always tinkling merrily all day long.

The saying that a Chinese would eat anything that moves may or may not be flippant; but as is with the world, one country's delicacies could be another's revulsion. This holds true for China as well. A Chinese would regard being labelled a "dog eater" as a derogatory insult. All the same, some Chinese in Southern China do enjoy eating dogs. Our Cambodian tourist guide salivate at the memory of the delicacies of dog meat.

I remember the occasion when a group of Vietnamese refugees in Darwin in the '70's was assured by kind Darwinians that they would be provided a good meal— hot dogs. Happiness all around till they set eye on the hot dogs—the revulsion on their faces was most memorable— they said: "We do eat dogs, but not THAT part of the dog!"

CHAPTER 3

MY MOTHER AND HER AUNTY PEONY

Today, I woke up with sharp memories of my mother which brings to mind something often chanted by my tolerant father and often echoed by my exasperated teachers in school—that a good girl will become a good woman, and a good woman will become a good wife. I really did not need this chant at all because I had a breathing example in my genteel mother. My mother left China when she was nine years old. She did not narrate much about the wrenching experience of being packed off with a distant relative (whom she addressed as "uncle" and a stranger from Southern China) to a faraway country known as Malaya, way, way across the foaming ocean. In fact, as far as I can remember, my mother did not seem to recollect much about her long sea voyage. She hardly ever talked about her biological parents and home in Southern China; much less about any siblings except that her two older sisters "had been given away" as well. Callous as this may seem to a Westerner, unfortunately this had been a familiar scenario with poor traditional Chinese families who had to "give away" some of their children in the hope that they could have a happier and more secure future.

I gathered that my mum's biological mother loved her dearly—there seemed no mention of a father which led me to the conclusion that her father must have died after she was born and her mother had to manage a farm all by herself to keep her family in clothes and food. That must have led to the need to parcel some of her children with relatives overseas to Malaya. The only inkling I have of my mother's past was the fact that she had been very, very ill when young and nursed to good health by a devoted mother. Mother was not one to exhibit her emotions; but there had been a catch in her voice when she mentioned how hard her mother had to slog from morn till dusk. As a young child, she did help in the farm as well as she could. One of the last acts of love in farewell was struggling with two buckets of water with the simple: "This is for you, Mother!" This farewell gesture was impregnated with an unutterable volume of love born of filial piety, the DNA of a traditional Chinese. Up to the end of her life, the fragrance of fresh coriander invoked a painful flashback— her two heavy buckets of water slung at both ends of the bamboo pole had swung too wildly which nearly brought about a nasty fall. This had been saved by her stumbling onto a bed of coriander bush. The fragrance of the crushed herb immediately projected two other images—the figure of a silent, stationary mother in black tunic and loose trousers by the fence and the strident cry "CHEH-CHEH . . . . h!" (S-I-S-T-E-R . . . r!") from her running young brother echoing after her when she rounded a bend of the road.

Mother brought up in the traditional Chinese way had never had the privilege of demonstrating her affection in physical term. The fact that she had spent her youth in a foster family could well have contributed significantly to the moulding of her character. I suspect that she had never known the pleasure of a hug in her life. Hers was a stoic stance which was the general current expectation of her time—physical demonstrations of affection had been discouraged—it was unfortunately seen as a weakness. Wonder how the term the "inscrutable Orientals" originated? Love and devotion should manifest through devotion and personal sacrifices. Kissing between parents had been a big NO NO; Not in public any way. This had been the practice of collective self-restraint of Confucius teaching.

What a terrible pity! Thank Goodness that our father had not been that emotionally-repressed—he loved caressing and fondling us children when we were young. One of the privileges of life today is the breakaway of this restrictive constraint; yes! Even among the inscrutable Orientals!! Chinese do love their children dearly. Very young children more often than not, bearing the pet name "Precious" had always been endlessly fondled and caressed. However, in my childhood days I seemed to recall that once the children reached their teens, physical fondling and kissing and any physical demonstration of love by any member of the family seemed to be an elusive dream! I remember distinctly how I had been ill in bed with a high fever when I was young and found mother by my bedside with an expression of loving concern. The minute she realized that she had been noticed, a mantle of embarrassment seemed to envelope her entire being—her expression suddenly changed to one of semi-aloofness and she left the room hurriedly in self-conscious embarrassment! What a pity that she had had such a sterile upbringing which had affected our own upbringing. We were desperately poor in my childhood days. My mother had a deep capacity for love, sacrifice and devotion up to the point of being a martyr. One of the rare pleasures that I had was to see mum's eyes sparkling with delightful excitement in the afternoons. At the back of our shophouse was a bakery and by about three in the afternoons, the heavenly aroma of freshly baked bread would send mother into raptures of delightful expectations. Seldom was a bearer of a loaf of fresh bread been welcomed with more glee. A slice of bread with butter and sprinkled with sugar was a salivating treat. Naturally, all of us, children, would dive in for our share and poor mother would always end up with the thinnest bit of leftover. It was normal that at meal times, our parents always reserved the best morsels for us.

My heart went out to her in knowing that in her "foster" family, she and another foster "sister" were the only two in a family of nine siblings who were uneducated. No blame inferred here! That the foster parents with a stringent income could only afford the best for their biological children was by no means an unnatural phenomenon; free education was non-existent then. One would find it hard to rival the blind love and devotion which my mother showered on her foster parents so naturally and happily. They had become her very own parents to love and to respect—the world of China shrouded in the misty past seemed to have evaporated with time. Did it? I don't know.

Such was her unconditional devotion to her foster mother that in later years, the latter had leant on her for support and company simply because mother had been her chief confidante. Mother's life-long love and devotion for her foster family had been pure and true. This was her characteristic attitude towards anyone who was kind to her and she had accepted as a friend. Both my parents shared this same characteristic—they were simple and genuine people who would repay any kindness or good deed double-fold. Mother's guiding principle in life seemed to gear on this deep capacity for sacrifice and a readiness to extend a helping hand to any and everyone who needed help. "Others before self" was her explicit motto in life so well expressed by Stephen Guellett:

> I expect to pass through this world but once.
> Any good thing, therefore, that I can do,
> Or any kindness I can show to any fellow human being,
> Let me do it now . . .
>
> Let me not defer,
> Nor neglect it
> For I shall not pass this way again.

Mother's sense of affiliation and closeness to this family swung her to adopt their practice and religion with unquestioning trust—she was a Catholic in practice but her foster mother for practical reasons had disallowed her from being formally accepted by the Church through baptism. The reason was simple—being a Catholic would have rendered her more inaccessible in the marriage market. Chinese Catholics were few and far between in British Malaya in those days.

My recollection of my mother's childhood home with her foster family is sparse and vague. I must have been about four or five years old when I first visited. Mother informed me that the physical aspect of everything seemed to be "the same". By the time of my visit, however, some of her siblings were living elsewhere through marriage.

The residence comprised two two-storey houses known as "shop-houses" in those days because the downstairs quarter was the "shop" the business quarter, while upstairs became the residential quarter. Shop-houses in those days were long, deep, spacious and with high ceilings. These two houses were interconnected both up and downstairs.

It had been a vast extended family with three generations living in claustrophobic proximity to each other, but surprisingly enough everyone seemed to be comfortable in each respective living-quarter. There were four of these for the four families.

The patriarch and august matriarch (quite a battle-axe from our father's description) would be living with their eldest son in the biggest quarter of the complex. My mother's foster mother, addressed as "first aunty" by my mother, and ("first grand-aunty" by us children) had a family of fifteen in their own living quarter. They had nine children of their own with 2 foster girls (mother and her companion "sister" from China), in addition to two unmarried sisters. The youngest sister was known as "Aunty Peony" to mother ("grand-aunty Peony" to us, children). I often wondered whether this vast family managed to have a cozy snuggle sardined in their quarter of four bedrooms and a fairly large living-room. Mother had three other "aunties" and "uncles" with their own families and they had their own quarters in this ancestral home.

Things could get woefully messy in the use of honorifics. In Chinese society, the siblings of one's parents would be addressed as "aunty" or "uncle" but a generation above this would be graduated to "grand-aunt" or "grand-uncle". The "grands" would be doubled "in greatness" with the rise of each generation. So the next generation above would be titled "great grand uncle" and "great, great grand . . ." etc. As if this was not sufficient torture for a poor child to remember, the honorific "Honourable" should precede the address on formal occasions such as New Year's greeting. So a "grand aunty" should be rightfully addressed as "Honourable grand aunty" accompanied by a respectful bow. I used to be quite in awe of these grand uncles and aunties being not quite sure whether it was a matter of personal appearances or the honorifics. My childish vision seemed to expect these multiple "greats" and "grands" would jack up the height of these august persons till their heads get lost in the clouds above.

The fun part comes when a man has more than one wife whose offspring would be addressed as "uncle" or "granduncle" by the generations below them. One of my friends' grandfather had five wives—the youngest of whom was YOUNGER than my friend who was in her late teens and she had to honour her younger step-grandmother, a mere slip of a girl with the honorific "grand-aunty". Grand-aunty's infant son had to be addressed as "uncle" In a large, extended family where one could have an exceptional randy grandpa, a situation could well arise when one's "great, grand-uncle" could be a mere infant.

In my mother's days, her foster uncles seemed to rule supreme in the house. Naturally the eldest uncle, the head of the household (after the old patriarch) seemed to have the importance of an object of worship. The ladies of the house had to bend almost double whenever they met any one of the uncles and it would be a boon indeed had they bothered to utter a reciprocal grunt to my muffled greeting. I should not really hold this against them, I suppose, simply because I fairly shrunk into the floor whenever I came across any of them; they all must have bad eyesight <u>and</u> bad hearing as well. I remember most clearly my "first grand-uncle"—his visage had always been that of a rigid, despotic stone-carving to this trembling child.

Just imagine hearing bits of conversation such as: "Yeah! grand-uncle is being breast-fed . . ." Wish I could have the delectable joy of piping out: "Grand-uncle! Come here! You need your bottom spanked!" Whoa! Delicious! What a feeling . . . ! Especially if the grand-uncle was the aloof "first uncle" of my mother's days!

Though each of the four families had its own private quarter, most of them appeared to eat their meals in the common kitchen. Meal times seemed to be the only times when one would come across other members of this vast extended family. This important kitchen-dining area was an L-shape room approximately six metres long and seven metres wide. Its major feature was a long wooden table with benches to accommodate about twelve diners at one time. Right opposite this long table was the kitchen, a simple affair of brick BBQ-like structure with four open fire places for cooking purposes. The bottom part of this structure was for storing purposes—firewood and coal. These wood-fire "stoves" were a common feature in those days. A row of shelves and two big food closets were conveniently adjacent to both the kitchen and the dining-table. A single bathroom and dish-washing area occupied the other end of the room.

The only toilet was way downstairs. It was a version of our Australian "long-drop"—an open bucket was not far below the open squat hole. I would imagine that the quarter occupied by the eldest son's family and the elderly parents must have their own flush toilet facilities.

The family diners amounted to about more than twenty in number on an ordinary day. Members of the families would just slip into a vacant seat; food was being continually replenished and everything seemed to hum smoothly and naturally. It went without saying that the patriarch and matriarch with the eldest son's family would be the first to grace the table. The cooks and kitchen-hands would do the honour of the last round. All three meals of the day had been cooked meals. The main meal of the day was dinner, which, at its minimum, would always include a soup, three main courses and rice. The men in the family never helped in the washing and cooking—not regarded as "manly" occupation in that era. I am rather surprised that in Malaysia today, some of my contemporaries, who are fairly "westernized" with an English education, continue to make their Asian husbands' coffees and wash their cups!

Mother and her companion "foster" sister, being the older siblings in the family, had to help out in the family chores.

The appearance of mother's legs did cause me to wince in sympathy pain. They seemed to be hard-wired with an intricate pattern of varicose veins which appeared like a veritable page of a detailed road map—well laced with multiple green rivers and lumpy gnarled purple little hillocks. They did give her much pain but I fancy that it was her vanity that caused her dear—she had to wear long pants and stockings even in the killing humidity of Darwin!

Life seemed to rotate around meals—mum would be up at 5.30 each morning and on her feet for much of the day. Marketing was not in her portfolio—young girls and unmarried women would not be encouraged to mingle in public without male company. Since mother was not a Catholic, she would have been deprived of that breather on Sundays as well, when the family attended Church service on foot. The Church was less than a quarter of a mile away and thanks to my mischievous father I had a hilarious picture of a family procession led by the majestic matriarch of the family, at whose appearance even the birds would break off chirping in mid-tune! It appeared that with so many young girls in tow, Madame General (a sterner version of an unsmiling Queen Victoria) was armed with a long umbrella with a sharp pointed end, and woe betides any amorous glance at the young ladies in tow, from any passer-by! She was garnished with a huge bun of hair plonked right on the top of her head, not unlike a cowpat; and this was skewered by a deadly weapon of a glinting hair-pin.

Sunday was a very special day indeed, for the young girls—it was a good day's outing. Sunday was not a good day for the cooks and kitchen-maids for it was on this auspicious day that the parish priest was invited to the house for dinner. I had the privilege to sample one of these important occasions when mother had been required to help in the cooking. When the Divine Being made his appearance, the ladies of the house seemed to genuflect and wonders of wonders! The grand-uncles' faces were creased with smiles! This had been a transfixing moment of my life! A frightening sensation trembled through my entire system which must be akin to that of a near-death experience!

Mother used to look forward to the return of her foster sisters from school. It was a pleasure to listen to their "tales of wonder and joy"—a recount of the day's activities in the big, wide world. Cocooned in her limited world I would imagine that to a child who had known no better, she would regard them as holding the key to the wondrous universe beyond the four walls. Mother had a happy childhood—the bond between her and her family had remained strong and close until death. Mother was an avid listener with an easy laughter. I can imagine what a happy group she and her five foster sisters had become. Life was so simple and tension-free for these happy children even in such a crowded house. Perhaps they were too young to remember, but mother, being the eldest sister, did share the tension of someone very dear to her—her best friend from a generation above her, her Aunty Peony, five years her senior.

When my mother talked about this aunty, she became a stranger in my eyes; an awesome demeanour seemed to transform her entire being and her voice was one of husky emotion. What I learnt from her was how the claustrophobic atmosphere of the house was killing her beloved aunty when escape seemed to be beyond her reach. This was not difficult for me to grasp especially after a few visits to the house in my childhood. The little township of mother's maiden home would perhaps have had about three to four thousand people with only three and a half streets; but this microcosm of life in the town's main street had been vibrant and noisy—everybody seemed to know everybody else. The most prominent person in town seemed to be my mother's Honourable first uncle who seemed to have inherited the major share of the family wholesale rice business, rubber plantations apart from many other obscure investments. He was also rumoured as being the local millionaire. It would be a very courageous person indeed, to dare to counter him. All mother's Aunty Peony yearned for was a meaningful future. She was the youngest daughter of one family in an austere household, and seemed to be a fish out of water in that stifling world which sun rose and set over an eternal round of meals and a life awash with idle, mundane matter. I can appreciate her feeling that her life-blood was being siphoned out of her by the day.

Mother's story has been engraved in my mind from the moment of her first utterance. It has become to me, a tale of beauty, of courage, of selfless devotion and pathos. It has poetic grandeur because it dealt with a young, intelligent girl who fit into the classic fable of the imprisonment of a beautiful, helpless maiden in distress. The heightened poignancy of this narrative has much to do with the fact that it involved my mother, a young 12-year-old, who had to witness and endure the agony of a slow death of a loved one. The devoted child-nurse's life force was not sufficient to stem the relentless ebbing of her aunty's life.

By the time of my childhood visits, mother's foster family members had dwindled from fifteen to eight. However, I was informed that the physical aspect of the world outside had not changed much at all. Eight adults of two generations jammed into four bedrooms was already a tight fit then—no wonder "Aunty Peony" in her time needed fresh air. The window which had been "aunty Peony's" favourite perch opened to an ever-shifting panorama of activities, noise and the ubiquitous heavy odour of spices intermingled with that of vegetation in various stages of ripening. There was the eternal clatter and chatter of pedestrians, rickshaws, bicycles, the occasional cars and trucks. Right below her window, the on-going hustle and bustle of sweaty shirtless coolies (labourers) loading and unloading sacks of rice and smelly sheets of rubber were a living testimony to the success of the family business. It was a marvel that this winding line of human ants bent double with their ponderous loads could still afford to throw raucous remarks at each other.

The main street which was a two-lane affair seemed to shrink in width when other carts and trucks were also busy loading and unloading their goods. All the heave-hoes and clamour mingled with the blaring music from the shops certainly made one envy the deaf. The musical cacophony was a mixture of Cantonese, Mandarin, Malay, English and Indian music. It must have been a merciful relief to many that the punk varieties that assault our ears today were not in competition then.

It certainly was a very musical township. Those who had a long-playing record would belt it out with gusto. Those who had no musical equipment to drive one insane did outclass in their own skill—the tinsmith shop round the corner had its own orchestra—bare-chested young men, four of them, sat on the concrete floor of their shop banging and clanging at all types of cooking wares with a very arresting tempo, They seemed to be dedicated acolytes in their art. The Indian barber shop right opposite mother's Aunty Peony's window had two speakers facing the street with the same three love songs on high volume for most part of the day. This shop certainly scooped up the first price for tenacity of effort to drown out all other competitors.

Now that both my parents are dead and gone, how I wish that I had not wasted the opportunities to know more about their world which could be as alien as another planet to me. I lay the blame on myself because wrapped up in my own life, it had not been my practice to spend more time with them. This is my eternal regret—"Youth is wasted on the young." Indeed!

Seventeen-year-old Aunty Delicate Peony, light of foot and trim of figure was a pensive beauty with jet black hair. Her black eyes always had a sad, wistful look which seemed to fasten steadily onto the far beyond—over the irregular tiled roof-tops, up, up and way yonder. My mother was a light, energetic girl of 12 and in spite of the age disparity, both girls had struck up a close friendship. Mother with two shiny expressive black eyes would preen with happy pride that the aloof and genteel aunty would care to notice her enough to spend time with her. This treasured companionship would give them the indulgence of a teacher-pupil relationship. It was her Aunty Delicate Peony who had taken the pains to teach mother the alphabet and my mother treasured the many delightful hours listening to stories read to her.

Her Aunty Delicate Peony had wanted to be a teacher. She had completed her O level (Year 10) in the local Convent. She had loved school, and she knew that further education could grant her that key to the treasure house of books which would transport her into a world of splendour and knowledge. There had been no public library of any kind in those days—and with the termination of her school-life, whatever books she could have had borrowed from the limited library of her school had been denied her. She had begged to further her education but that would entail her attending an institution in the city quite some distance from her town. This turned out to be an impossible dream—the city would seem to be as accessible as that far out in the galaxy.

The problem would have been more than finance—each member of the family had a monthly allowance from the Central Bank, the Patriarch. She and her sisters (being daughters) would have a relatively insubstantial inheritance compared to what the sons in the family would inherit; but then, all her sisters had rallied together with offer of financial support. It was her bad luck that her father, the old patriarch, their only surviving parent, had been away in China at this point in time. Permission for such an "audacious" request would have to be granted by the acting-head of the family—her eldest brother. That it was not a regular practice for girls to be well-educated was in this case a lame excuse—her powerful eldest brother had allowed his own daughter to be trained as a teacher. My mother had been vague about the real reason why permission had been brutally denied her Aunty Delicate Peony. Her pleas had fallen on deaf ears, so were her sisters'. Her brother's "NO!" had been as deadly final as the thud on the neck of the guillotined victim!

Aunty Delicate Peony's out-pouring of sorrow and pain to a little devoted 12-year-old was not a sufficient safety valve to sustain her. She took the only course opened to her—a hunger strike. No members of her immediate family, her three sisters' and my mother's tears could shake her determination. Another special envoy had been sent—the stone sculpture was unmoved—he did not even relent enough to go over to check how weak his youngest sister had become.

The faithful 12-year-old nurse who had crouched on the floor by her bedside day and night had her first lesson on the travail of the slow death of a loved one. Mother held her thin hands; she stroked them, she caressed them in her frantic attempt to coax some life and colour into the limp fingers. In dismay, they noticed that her parched lips got bluer by the day; her eyes had ceased to flutter open even ever so briefly. Mother lamented that she would be happy to attend to the hygiene of her incumbent aunty day and night, if only, if only she would hold on, just hang on there! The child-nurse had prayed that by clutching her aunty's hand, her own life-force would flow to the limp body if only to keep her from slipping away so relentlessly; anything, anything just to gain time for . . . . ? They had all hoped that perhaps, just perhaps, the Old Patriarch would return soon . . . . Sorrow and pain numbed the little nurse's nerves; but the clamour of everyday living still filtered into her consciousness—yes, life was flowing by in relentless normalcy. Gradually the spirit of the gentle, elegant girl with the flowing black hair slipped away out of her window at last—up and up over the ragged roofs of the noisy shops across the road, accompanied by the crass, abrasive street music . . . .

Such was the authority of the head of the family! The patriarch returned home too late to make his decision known. Mother said that the old man went into a fearful rage and didn't he perform? He clutched a cleaver and old as he was, it appeared that he dashed after his eldest son and heir through the house with dramatic fervour. This time, his sisters over whom he had ruled with such brutality had to beg the Honourable father to spare his life.

Life is full of "What-ifs". What if the austere father had been approached instead for permission? What if he had returned home on time? What if . . . .

> The Moving finger writes; and, having writ,
> Moves on; nor all thy piety nor wit
> Shall lure it back to cancel half a Line,
> Nor all thy Tears wash out a word of it.
> (*The Rubaiyat of Omar Khayyam, Verse 51*).

CHAPTER 4

IN WALKED FATHER

The exact detail of how father bumped into the path of my cloistered mother had been vague to me. I think what occupied my astonished mind was the startling discovery that father seemed to be one of the very few who could manage to crumple the face of mother's "Honourable First Uncle" into a smile which appeared to be a jagged gash on an eyeless face. This could only be explained by the fact that the rare act of smiling so shocked his small eyes that they shrivelled into two tight slits.

This "Honourable First Uncle"—(The Wall, to me) being the eldest son and heir of an extended family had always been a figure of majesty and forbidding severity to everyone I came across. His sisters and the entire women folk in the family had the habit of moving aside seemingly to genuflect when they met him. Naturally, as a child, I was terrified of him especially when he seemed to smell of moth balls.We children had to bow in his presence and address him as "Honourable Grand First Uncle" and would count ourselves honoured to hear a near imperceptible grunt from somewhere up the wall.

"The Wall" was only about five-foot-ten, an expressionless figure whose little round gold-rimmed glasses enhanced his severity although he always seemed to appear dapper in his loose white flannel suit. The row of bronze buttons on his coat in rigid attention seemed to mesmerize me into avoiding looking up his face. His neatly combed carpet of silver hair lent an air of austerity as forbidding as the sanctity of his expansive office. Father, always addressed politely as "Teacher" by "the Wall" would be shown to a swivel chair in the holy of holies of the god.

How this transpired was beyond me; the story had been vague. What I heard from my father was that he had done the "Honourable first uncle" a favour when father was a young man, and that had saved the uncle from potential financial ruin. Father had been vague on this matter to his children. Mum had been acquainted with the full detail of course; but when asked by me for more detail, she brushed off the affair with "There had been some unfortunate accident . . ." I believe that father must have been invited to the case as an arbiter. As usual, Chinese, especially the Chinese in those days would fight shy of litigation; they would strive to solve the matter amicably and in private over endless cups of tea. What I remember was that my naïve father had offered to take a gamble with his own reputation; he was prepared to accept the consequences should the worst transpire. It appeared that the Arthurian knight magnanimously proffered this sacrifice because he, my father, had claimed that he had no family attachment in Malaya and his fall from grace would not be as disastrous as that of the uncle, the son of a well-known family in town and which family name should not be besmirched at any cost!

It was just so much like father to rush in embrace of the Arthurian gallantry so readily and impulsively. I had always wondered how the only bread-winner of a dependent family in China came to take that gamble.

The outcome of this petrifying gamble ended like a fairy-tale—father's arbitration must have been riding on the wings of magic—all had been amicably and happily solved. The finale of this drama was what I enjoyed most—Father, the hero, was formally invited to the Family Ancestral Hall where a formal tea-ceremony took place. The entire huge family of the two shop-houses which had suffered the tragic demise of an intelligent girl stood behind a seated, brocade-clad patriarch facing my father who was sitting opposite the entire family in a beautifully carved red, cedar wood chair.

The old man began with a speech of thanks to my father with an offer of a cup of tea. A formal tea ceremony like this is a sacred affair. If tea was offered by a senior to a junior (the old man was in his eighties, and father was in his mid-thirties), it certainly signified a momentous gesture of great honour to my father and an acknowledgement of an enduring debt from the entire family.

He then summoned the "Honourable first uncle" who nearly brought about a disaster to the family to kowtow to father with the offer of a cup of tea to father. The litany was to the effect that he and his family offered their gratitude and thanks for father's noble effort. He also formally reiterated what the old man had promised—that as long as he and his father were alive, my father's "rice bowl would never be empty." It was a sacred promise that as long as the patriarch and the man who my father had rescued from some dire consequence were alive, my father and his family would be financially secure. This sacred promise to my father eventuated in an interest-free loan of about sixteen thousand dollars to my father to build his house.

Then, the grand present—they offered my mother, an innocent "gem of the household" to be his wife. Mother had great faith and love for her foster mother and I am sure innocent, naïve and self-effacing as she was, she was happy to follow her esteemed foster parents' advice. Mother knew nothing about the big, frightening world outside. She was only a slight, timid girl about five feet four inches in height. I used to tease her that I had the privilege of "looking down upon her" since I am about an inch taller than her. Her best features were her sparkling dark eyes which lit up her whole personality with her ready laughter. Mother was twenty-one years old when she married my father who was seventeen years her senior. Suffice it to say that the marriage had lasted. It lasted not because my mother was a fabulous cook and dedicated housewife but that a marriage was regarded as sacred and meant to last for life. I believe that mother had been advised by her foster mother that father was an ideal match for at least two major reasons—he was a person revered by the family and they were certain that he would take good care of her. The other practical reason was the assurance that since the family would be living in Malaya, mother would be safe from the "clutch" of any "bullying" members of the in-laws. There had been enough anecdotes about such bullying to encourage women to enter a Convent and embrace a life of chastity.

What did Confucius, the great Sage have to say about men and women?

"Man is the representative of Heaven and is supreme over all things. Woman yields obediently to the institutions of man and helps him to carry out his principles. On this account she can determine no thing (sic) of herself, and is subject to the rule of the three obediences. When young, she must obey her father and elder brother; when married, she must obey her husband; when her husband is dead, she must obey her sons. She may not think of marrying a second time."[*1]

Women in modern China today have come a long, long way indeed.

From father's standpoint, he had done the right thing—he had written to China for permission to take a second wife since a filial son was expected to produce at least a male heir to the family. This father had excelled!

The Ying and Yang in this marriage had been complementary—mother, the Ying, (the shade) was docile and respected her husband. Father the Yang (the light) was the epitome of a manly man. This seemed to be his credo for life—the man, the strong one should be the head of his family who are always under his protective wings. He, the head of the family would assume full responsibilities for their well-being. The man occupied the driver seat which has only room for one. He was lucky that his wife, a wise and introspective person was fully aware of this. She was truly grateful that the family always came first in her husband's life and he loved spending his time with the family.

Father somehow managed to forge his way ahead in this terrible time of the world's Great Depression. I can still hear father gurgling with pride when visitors praised him for the good upbringing of his brood of children. There were seven of us out of a crop of thirteen! Poor mother! Parents in those days had to stumble through life blindly. They had never known the existence of contraceptives— they were probably non-existent then. Sex education, infant care, post-natal education and all types of aids, education, consultation etc. that we are so lucky to take for granted had been undreamt of! How brave and fantastic were our pioneer forefathers!

My mother was only twenty-three, straight out of the cocoon of a very sheltered life when she gave birth to me. It must have been a horrendous experience for one whose knowledge of sex revolved round the belief that one's offspring literally springs from somewhere, sometime, when a man kissed her on the forehead. My father, nearly twice her age, must have been regarded as a father-figure who was a mobile encyclopaedia with all the answers to her queries and doubts. She respected him highly.

In an age devoid of sex education and a salacious diet on romantic stories, which our current teenagers, (compliments of technological advancement) enjoy, the very experience of carrying a baby must have been a terrifying discovery. Her expert medical advisor and midwifery manual was her foster mother whose sage advice she devoured with unquestioned faith. On the issue of pre-birth care to facilitate an easy birth, mother was to studiously remember the dictum SQUAT. Yes, she had been advised to squat, as often as possible. Yes,

SQUAT—don't sit, don't bend in any daily chores—just SQUAT. The reward would be a smiling replica of herself some months later.

Smiling indeed! I was told that she had a terrifying and painful first birth. Labour pain had started 24 hours earlier, then—me! my squalling and screaming loud enough to drown the crash of a collapsing world must have impressed upon her that this was what the trauma of the end of the world was like. What was even more dramatically spectacular was that my poor father who had piously kow-towed to his revered ancestors to let him offer them a son had lost face! Father, in a demented frenzy of shame and disappointment was for tossing me, the "useless female" under the bed.

Mother cried, her foster mother cried in unison, so did the midwife—fearing possibly that she might not be paid for her service. I was told that the timely tearful intervention of the august MIL—mother-in-law did manage to reduce my sentence. Father screeched to an abrupt brake and consoled himself that he would give away this bundle of shame after the important one-month post natal convalescence.

I often wondered what speeches he had to make to his ancestors for loving me.

I presume that I should consider myself lucky to be born in a "modern era" when sex education was available in a Convent school. This privilege was available only to the Senior students in the last year of High School, our Year 10 level.

The abiding memory of the lesson on sex and reproduction education was my naïve wonder about the special hushed atmosphere in the class. We had to sit ramrod straight with our hands demurely folded on the desk in front of us. It was an awe-inspiring moment indeed—the august Mother Superior was going to be our instructor! I was too focussed on her tomato-red face to comprehend what she was muttering in between her humming and coughing.

When her Holiness pointed with a cane to her masterpiece on the board, things became more confused—the diagram seemed to depict a sun-dried toad splattered on the ground with a couple of loopy things dangling about. There was what seemed to be some kind of a disfigured thumb sticking somewhere. That was our illuminating lesson on sex and reproduction. At the conclusion of the lesson, we dutifully stood to attention and uttered with awesome respect: "Thank you, Reverend Mother."

How did each preceding generation cope without what we have the privilege to enjoy today? Even as late as my parents' time, there were no washing-machines for a start and how my mother had to cope with one baby in arm, another one crawling around and heavy with a third; in addition to being responsible for household chores on a tight budget defies understanding. This scenario certainly would be a nightmare that everyone wishes to wake up from. I do remember, however, that father managed to have a servant and maid in times of need. In spite of the fact that we had employed helpers, the abiding memory was of a very busy mother. This was especially so when we did have a very good-natured old servant once who was an appalling cook. So the scenario was of mother being the last person left to eat lukewarm left-over meals.

I don't remember my mother ever crying with frustration or misery, but there had been one heart-wrenching cry that I remember too well—another of her babies, a boy, had died after a few months from birth. Mother's pain was poignant when she asked: "why does God make me carry the child for all the nine months when He means to take him away after birth?" Three of the baby girls had been "given away" to father's good friends for dual reasons—I would imagine that my parents could not cope with having a child each year and they believed that the girls would have a chance of a better life with their adopted parents.

Father naturally had the same dream as everyone else. He had wanted to own his own home after years of renting premises. His dream-home materialized in the mid-fifties and it had a flushed toilet, his pride and joy! My feeling was one of mingled amusement and embarrassment when father, in his guided tour to our guests, would march them to the toilet. "See! One tug here and everything disappears!" With folded arms across his chest and a beautific smile all over his face, father's profound announcement befitted the miracle he could perform.

Our new house was a modest, average "shop-house" of the day. It had two storeys, the top storey was rented out, and we lived on the entire ground floor. The front part of the building which is normally used as a shop section (as is common in the S.E Asian countries today) was divided into two sections. The formal sitting-room occupied the front section while its second half was subdivided into two bedrooms. The big master bedroom was situated in the living quarters at the back of the building. This was also the utility area which comprised the kitchen, toilet, bathroom and dining area.

I was still in High School then. During the family's first grand tour of the house, father proudly announced to me: "This is your room!" There was only one bed in the room and father continued: "This is your bed!" Being the only proper bed in the house, that room became the girls' bedroom. My three sisters had been given the privilege to sleep on mats on the floor in "my room"

The vision of a very smug and proud father in his first new home had extended beyond the toilet. His suite of a five-piece sitting-room furniture was his other exhibit. That was the popular stumpy suite of the day—four timber chairs in majestic attendance round an equally clunky, heavy timber coffee table. There were four blue cushions on the chairs which were off-limit to the family—only visitors had the privilege of warming the cushions. Father, confined to the house in his blindness would only seat himself on a punishing straight-back wooden chair throughout the day

But alas! Father did not live long enough to enjoy his new house. When father passed away all too soon, true to the sacred promise at the tea ceremony, "as long as they were alive, my father's rice bowl would never be empty . . ." Honourable first uncle sent his son to request for the balance of the loan—12,000.00 Straits dollars, even before my father was cold in the coffin. The operative words seemed to be "as long as our father was alive . . ."

Mother suddenly widowed at the age of forty-eight without her crutch and with a string of young children in tow begged for more time. Request was refused and the next thing we knew, mother had collapsed and was carted off for an urgent surgery for hysterectomy. She seemed to be still in shock for quite some time but managed to claw back to health and to face the reality of three more door-knockings for "immediate payment of balance of the loan". A respected family friend of the Honourable Uncle and family sallied forth with my mother to appeal for more time—all in vain. The stone wall never budged an inch—the chiselled gash in the wall had never appeared in our presence.

Rattling in my ear was the joke which my wicked father related about one of the occasions he had tea with the Honourable first uncle. It appeared that the stone wall had gushed about how grateful he and his family were to father, that the family would never be able to pay father enough—father was worth his weight in gold. Father joked that he would not say "no" to the gift of a solid gold monkey (he was born in the year of the monkey); but that he would appreciate more to have a solid gold ox since his wife was born in the year of the ox.

*2 The little girl with the page-boy haircut with
her mum, siblings, servant & maid.

CHAPTER 5

"THERE COMES A TIME IN OUR LIVES WHEN THE INNOCENCE OF SPRING IS A MEMORY"

Whenever I return to Australia from overseas, I never cease to appreciate the wonderful, clear blue sky, the fresh air and the immense open space, which complements her big-hearted people. How lucky can we be—Australians are kind, friendly people with a unique brand of humour and a sense of fun which never ceases to fascinate me.

I have been very lucky in having beautiful and helpful neighbours especially in my current residence in Brisbane. A couple whom I fell in love with at first sight was Ian and Debbie. They called in one day, uninvited, when I was weeding in the garden.

"Can I help you?"

A chirrupy voice floated from behind the gardenia shrub. Out appeared the owner of the voice—a three-and-a-half-foot tall lady with burning blue eyes and a cute blonde ponytail. Debbie was accompanied by her little brother with a dark brown moustache. Ian, the moustachioed gentleman was a stocky three-footer rather squarish in shape and as graceful as a tin soldier. Ian was less timorous and wanted to show me his new T shirt which boasted of a garish monster across his barrel chest.

"Daddy got me this today."

He smiled broadly and his crescent moon of a dark brown moustache curved generously upwards to point to his prominent ears. Ian's vegemite-coated slice of bread bore evidence where the rest of the curved chunk had travelled to.

When I asked Ian how old he was, he spread his out the fingers of his fat, spatula hand and said: "Five!"

His helpful sister quickly asserted her seniority with "And I am his big sister! I am six!"

Both were unselfconsciously at home even when I turned down their request to help me. Debbie skipped about the garden while Ian acquainted me with the list of toys he had at home. They visited me often, but unfortunately, in selfish self-defence, I had to decline their help to protect valuable plants from being treated as weeds. This never deterred their good will towards me, however. On one of these visits, Ian's exhibit was his pride and joy—a brand new red tricycle which was his birthday present. He chivalrously invited me to have a ride and forgave me magnanimously for a miserable failure when my knees decided to go on strike—they were stubbornly jammed on the ground.

I had a great respect for these two. They never gave up their offer of help which I had always selfishly declined.

Debbie's offer was to help me with "any washing up to be done in the house?" Ian's, was to protect me from spiders. He helpfully suggested that these could be in my bedroom, perhaps? They always had something to do—Debbie loved skipping about and picking up the river-polished pebbles to build patterns and Ian cycled about the yard in between pressing their noses against the French windows to peer inside the house.

It never occurred to stupid me how utterly curious they were about my living quarters until one day, they turned up at the door with a posey of flowers and their heart-melting smiles. I happened to be having friends over for lunch and I regret to this day that I had failed to invite them in as well. It only occurred to me long after they were gone that they might have wondered what strategy my guests had employed to be admitted into the house.

How amiable these lovely children had been! I enjoyed their simple pleasure and garrulity. When the family moved out, they called in with another posey neatly tied—

"From mum's garden," Debbie volunteered. "We are moving house . . ."

"Far away!" Ian fixed me with his big, brown eyes. "We cannot come to see you again."

I miss them! They personified the beauty and purity of children. I miss them! It's been more than ten years since I had the privilege of their friendship. What a magical world children live in! One would hope that beautiful children should be left to remain in their magic world for as long as changes of time can allow. They would be well into their teens now and in this fast changing 21st century of progress, I hope teenagers like these two would always remain lovably communicative with their parents and not to retreat too far into their exclusive virtual world of cyber space where non-peer group such as parents are not welcome.

Our two-income families today have contributed much to weakening family bonding, sadly eroded by the ubiquitous televisions and computers which often are not ideal baby-sitters. What a waste of good opportunities when sensibly and wisely monitored, these could be such valuable educators!

More often than not, devotees of the screen culture are fed on a diet of action-programmes liberally garnished with blood, gore, fast cars and explicit sex scenes. Often, multiple loud, fast actions piling upon one another proffer a surreal world of a video film on fast forward. I often wonder if this frenetic action-pack mode is necessary because the attention span of the viewers is too short? And they must remain captivated at all cost? What seems especially worrying is the matter of role models. Some people, especially the impressionable young often tend to deify people on the public stage—examples are sports heroes, favourite film personnel, just to name a few. If these adopted "role models" are closely associated with anti-social behaviour liberally garnished with unsavoury language, no wonder it is "cool" to be seen to do the same.

Some of these adopted "role models" can do no wrong— "Orange Juice"—O.J. Simpson comes to mind. His sporting prowess seemed to be his invincible armour that could protect him even from a possible case of murder. If the likes of Michael Jackson can bleed the hearts of millions of worshipful mourners worldwide, I think we should take a hard look at our education system and the power of the media.

I often wonder if it is a case that the real world is so untenable that we come across people who need to be wired to escape to another world, a two-dimensional virtual world of cardboard characters? Into a world of primitive heart-pounding loud music some of which has proven to be effective instrument of torture banned under the UN Convention Against Torture. If direct interaction with humankind is the breeding ground for sensitivity and empathy, it was no wonder that the SQUAWK from my incredulous father in the dream was so unnerving.

I am inclined to count myself lucky to be a child of "that other age", that of the 20th century when I was very lucky to be able to remain in the fairy floss cocoon of childhood magic and innocence for that long. The pace of living then was relatively sane and slower; the adhesive of family bonding and personal interactions had contributed much to character-building. One of the most valuable gifts of that time was the opportunity to live out the beautiful world of innocence enriched by the food of imagination, which was as nectar to the gods. That was at a time when we children had the opportunity to roam about in safety and parents did not have to snatch their children from school, overcome with anxiety when they did not appear at a prescribed time. We did not have to lock our doors; and strangers, more often than not, had been met with a smile.

Litanies such as "I AM BORED" seemed to be unknown. The loneliest of children such as Beatrice Potter, had exploited her imagination to the full to humanise the enduring animals which were her companions. The Brontë sisters in a lonely world of the forbidding heath, enriched each other's life with their creative world of imagination which has been immortalised in the Classics

Childhood for me was an adventurous wonder about my surroundings. I remember being curious about how the time on the clock was never the same, the sly hands on the clock were to be blamed! When did they slide away without being noticed? So one day, this five-year-old sleuth decided to catch the devious clock for "cheating" on her. I slithered on my belly across the room to sit in silence under the table with my eyes fixed on the clock on the wall opposite. It was a matter of importance to me to catch the moment when the hands of the clock would surreptitiously spurt ahead.

Kindergartens seemed to be a non-existence then; the official school age was seven. The Japanese Occupation had robbed me and my generation of an early education; I started school late. We children owed much of our early childhood education to our father when he returned from work each day.

The earliest memory I had of my father was his cuddling me and comforting me with: "you are safe now! Papa is here!" What captivated my attention at that moment was a surprise that I was yawning! I must be about three or four years old then and was most puzzled how this came about—after all, didn't I just wake up from a deep sleep?

Surely people don't yawn after a sleep? It seemed to appear that I had just come out of a crisis—the high fever had mercifully subsided.

The father who was so demonstrative with his children was a short, squarish, sturdy man of about five feet ten with a bulging forehead and receding hairline. There was a smell of antique books about him which I found fascinating. I had been led to believe that a bulging forehead is a sign of great intelligence. Needless to say, a daily check in the mirror became a compulsory chore which always ended with a comfortable assurance—yes, my forehead was bulging all right—very slowly of course.

It was father's walk that characterized him—and what a walk! Not unlike George Bush's Texan swagger. Father believed that a man must be firm, strong, and manly; one could not mistake the sound of his firm footsteps from afar. This complemented his firm handshakes naturally and a deep baritone voice to boot. He was one who did not need the use of a microphone at a public speech. Father was a big notice box. He loved public speaking. This became his unofficial profession when he was in demand to arbitrate in family feuds and to conduct important occasions such as weddings and funerals. Observation of Confucian rites had been obligatory at such times and father's role was therefore more than that of a Master of Ceremony. It was naturally "not done" to discuss payment at all for such service. The custom was to deliver a red packet, cash payment in a red envelope as a form of financial "token" of gratitude and thanks on happy occasions and a white packet (in a white envelope) on sad occasions. Such "tokens" were often generous and quite substantial. The offering families could not afford "to lose face".

Father's eloquence and ready quotations from the Classics and apt performance of Confucian rites could make one laugh or cry spontaneously. His bubbling sense of humour and a biting sarcasm never failed to whip up a ripple of laughter across the room. I suspect that it was his apt quotations from the Confucian Classics and his

easy eloquence that enthralled his audience. In such moments of poetic grandeur, his name Li Yünyen—a rough translation could mean "craggy cliff behind clouds" which brings to mind this Chinese brush painting of a scholar communing with nature—a craggy cliff veiled in a gossamer of cloud. It seems an apt picture to epitomise my nature-loving father. How else could I fit that name to the man who held so steadfast to integrity and principles in life and yet could embrace such a haunting sensitivity to the splendour of nature?

*1 Scholar and cliffs behind clouds

It was at a close friend's funeral when his eulogy produced a gush of tears from the kneeling members of the family and some unabashed sniffling from the spectators. What I understood was that tugging one's heartstrings was the expected thing to do on such a sad occasion. He was a much sought-after Master of Rites for all occasions. It was on occasions like this that father felt he was ten-foot tall. Not so, on another memorable occasion. It was at a school concert—father was a librarian of this Chinese school. His Mandarin, heavily flavoured with a distinctive Teochew accent would itself be a matter of laughter apart from his clowning on stage. After the concert, father announced to me that he was elated not only because of the positive reaction of the audience but also that he heard someone alluding to him as "the chief clerk". In the Cantonese dialect, it means the "Big Boss".

Little seven-year-old me piped in with tactless candour that what the speaker meant was the "big teapot"—an allusion to his Texan swagger. Father's elbows sticking out from the sides of his body did remind one of the handles of a teapot. The term for such a disastrous difference in meaning was the fault of a slight turn of pitch and tone. Father's sagging jaw seemed to be in danger of touching his chest. The seven-year-old girl was, for the first time aware of a very human man with endearing childlike qualities.

Young father left home because of poverty. China was in bad shape; the ravaging Japanese had been a bully and a threat to peace. Father, being the eldest son of three deemed it his responsibility to find succour for his extended family. He had too many mouths to feed—the two-generation family comprised his parents and two younger brothers; his wife and two daughters. If migration was the only salvation for his family, then he had no alternative but to leave home secretly one day. I can still see the sadness in his eyes when he recounted how he had to endure sea-sickness in the dark under-deck of a ship. The vision of an agonizing family believing that he had abandoned them gave him the strength to endure the impossible—he lived for the day when he could let his grieving family know that succour was at hand—that he, the eldest son had survived overseas to look after them. He just had to surmount the insurmountable for the simple reason that he was the lifeblood of his extended family and Confucius' idea of filial piety was indeed his lifeblood.

Father had to exile himself for the simple reason that there seemed no hope in a humiliated China which not only had been overrun by Colonial Powers from the West but the country was starving from the marauding Japanese. Japan occupied Mongolia in 1933 and created a puppet state in five provinces in China in 1935. By December 1937, Japan had overrun Nanjing and in a seven-week spree massacred tens of thousands of civilians and fugitive soldiers. At least 20,000 women had been raped. Foreign press labeled this "The Rape of Nanking." Father was just one of the thousands of Chinese who had chosen to migrate overseas to seek a more secure future for their families. These migrating die-hards are known as "Overseas Chinese". Their only life-line in their new venture lay in the intricate network of benevolent Chinese groups who helped with limited funds and assistance with job-seeking.

The "network" which opened a new world to father landed him in British Malaya. The eternal British again!! British Malaya was a challenging world for a non-English educated. Overseas Chinese had to live on their wits and through their own benevolent associations funded by Chinese philanthropists. Father had lived on his wits all right. I remember his public persona more than the actual occupation he was in. Other than being the Master of Rites and Ceremonies, his base seemed to be varied—he had always been associated with assisting the running of various businesses. At one point in his life, he had been adviser and librarian of a big Chinese school. However, he did own a small grocery shop with one employee for a few years.

I remember this employee quite well, a lanky man of about twenty-five with a shock of black curly hair—au natural! Not permed, all very unusual for a Chinese. What struck me most about him were his goldfish eyes; he certainly had big, alert protruding eyes which compensated for his lack of communication. His main work was to transport grocery stock to and from our shop with the help of a big tricycle, which was actually a bicycle propelling a trailer attached to its front. This form of goods carrier is still popular in S.E. Asian countries today. "Gold Fish" brought an end to father's entrepreneur venture after acquainting himself with father's "trade secret" and had the audacity to open his own grocery store right opposite ours with a better discount of goods! Father's business venture would seem doomed from the start anyway, thanks to his hungry children who were adept at helping themselves to the numerous sweetmeats and biscuits. We were too engrossed in our daily thievery to realize that we were objects of great amusement to all our neighbours.

Father had been a very active man in his life; one of the hats he wore was that of an executive officer of the

Teochew Benevolent Association which position he held till blindness came in his way. He used to sing hymns of praise about many outstanding philanthropists who had monuments built in grateful memory of them. The numerous hospitals and schools built by these saviors were a living testimony of their contribution to the social welfare of the Overseas Chinese. Everyone admires the person who trades home security for the future good of his family. Tales of penniless Chinese migrants who became wealthy philanthropists in father's day were numerous. "The rags to richness" tag was an everlasting badge of pride and honour to many such philanthropists throughout British Malaya, Singapore and indeed in farther climes! Living monuments such as family temples and mansions still dot the S.E. Asian landscape.

One such is the "Cheong Fatt Tze Mansion" in Georgetown, present-day Penang in Malaysia. Mr Cheong arrived penniless in Malaysia from Southern China at the age of sixteen and slaved away to become one of the most colourful personalities with a vast financial empire. He was dubbed "one of China's last mandarins and first capitalists". Such was his fame that the Dutch and British authorities had their flags flown at half mast throughout the colonies on his death in 1916.

The elaborate "Cheong Fatt Tze Mansion" known as "La Maison Bleu" stands loud and proud today being the winner of the Architectural Award for Conservation. This flamboyant building has thirty-eight rooms, five courtyards, seven staircases and two hundred and twenty windows. It is not unusual for servants and cleaners of such edifices to be literally on the move throughout the year dusting and cleaning from one end to the other. What I found amusing was the existence of secret passages in some of these showpieces which were used by the Lord and Master of the house in his nocturnal visits to some maids' chambers.

Unfortunately, not every Chinese was a giving philanthropist who played such a crucial role as these overseas Chinese. At the other end of the spectrum were numerous others whose reputation had besmirched the family name for generations to come. If "all the perfumes of Arabia" could not sweeten the little hands of the conscience-stricken Lady Macbeth, there is not a dewdrop chance in Hell for those without a conscience to cleanse their reputation throughout history. Such scum of the earth included one Wu Binjian touted as the alleged richest Chinese in the world in 1834, during China's most painfully humiliating time in History. Wu had built his financial empire on the blood and suffering of his fellowmen—his wealth flourished from the iniquitous Opium Trade which brought about the collapse of the Middle Kingdom. His other businesses—tea, silk and usury contributed to his investment in the building of the American Railway System. Father seemed to froth at the mouth when he touched upon such human parasites. He endorsed what the great Sage, Confucius had said, that one's good reputation is more important than all the wealth in the world; it, the reputation would live on after death. The stench of a bad reputation will saturate posterity . . .

Tales of patriotism and sacrifice abounded in father's historical dramatization in his family kindergarten class where I was one of its most attentive students. Chinese civilization with its entire splendour and grandeur had gone through centuries of turbulence, bloodshed and disasters. In times of adversity, there would emerge unusual persons to face the challenge. Personal integrity, courage and sacrifice had produced a fair crop of heroes and heroines. Memories of such people had been fondly celebrated through stories and especially, the Beijing Opera. It must be remembered that oral transmission of their heroism down the generations would tend to be romanticized and being embellished with mythologies and legends, fact could easily be merged with fictions.

Historically, the Chinese have a habit of deifying such great persons, especially those who had suffered and died in the cause of patriotism. They are immortalized through the monuments and temples that are scattered throughout China, some even spreading far across S.E. Asia.

The little girl's mental filing cabinet had a special niche for Yue Fei (岳飛) a statuesque warrior of the Northern Song era (960-1126 AD) Though born into an impoverished family, Yue Fei managed to get a First Degree in the Imperial Examination. His military skill had also earned him a formidable reputation. This scholar-general was most feared by the Jin barbarian horde which he soundly defeated in 1140AD. Yue Fei, with his burning love and loyalty to the Chinese civilization regarded the Jurchins (who formed the Jin Empire) as another barbarian horde to be kept out of China Proper at all costs.

His patriotism was literally branded into his back. History varied regarding who tattooed his back with the famous "Patriotism to Fatherland".

Be it his wife or mother, father's detail of the numerous needle punctures on the skin rubbed in with vinegar to ensure that the tattoo was well burnished into his flesh brought to life the student's own private tattoo torture. During the sewing classes with her mother, the needle would steadfastly decide to play the vanishing game unless the left hand remained its home and pincushion.

But alas! Qin Hui (秦檜) who became Prime Minister in 1131, had this patriot beheaded on a trade-off with the Jin horde to promote his own interest. Qin Hui had earned himself two nick names. One was "Stinker" and the other was "deep-fried devil" a strip of deep-fried dough which Chinese consume with relish, especially when dunked in strong coffee for breakfast. So consuming is the hatred of this man that the Chinese want his flesh to be eternally fried in deep oil as punishment; and of course, to the pragmatic Chinese, "waste not, want not," the deep-fried dough makes a scrumptious breakfast! Naturally, the ardent student felt that she too had to do her bit to contribute towards the ideal of patriotism. However, maturity in adulthood seemed to point a tantalizing finger towards wholemeal bread.

Father of course, chose this juncture to remind his students that a good reputation is more valuable than all the wealth in the world. This view is endorsed by the

English poet, George Herbert (1593-1632) in his poem, "Virtue" which began with:

> Sweet day, so cool, so calm, so bright,
>> The bridal of the earth and sky,
>> The dew shall weep thy fall to-night;
>>> For thou must die.

and ended with:

> Only a sweet and virtuous soul,
>> Like seasoned timber, never gives;
>> But though the whole world turns to coal,
>>> Then chiefly lives.

Statues of Yue Fei have been found in various parts of China. He has been deified; his temple and mausoleum are found in Hangzou. In a mark of eternal hatred of the Stinker, statues of the kneeling Qin Hui and his conniving wife are erected beside Yue Fei's statues. At the Hangzou mausoleum, there are four kneeling figures beside Yue Fei's-Qin Hui and his three accomplices had to pay eternal penance for their shame.

Mindful of the Sage's advice that example is the best teacher, father always tried to do so by living up to his historical role models, which meant, the students, too, had to prove their worth with excellent behaviour. This was not too appetizing to us; we preferred his other teaching method more—dramatized episodes in history and feats of historical heroes. The more we lapped up his histories, the more entertaining father became. Father's other favourite patriot was Wen Tianxiang, (1236-1283), another hero in the Southern Song era (1127-1279 AD). Like Yue Fei, Wen was also a Scholar-General who was responsible for keeping the barbarian hordes off China Proper. It appeared that the Song Dynasty had a difficult time keeping Genghis Khan and the Mongol horde from the Great Wall of China. The Mongols, a formidable force, fresh from their conquest of Russia and Japan had admired the great General Wen, who, they came to believe, was an impediment to their victory. It became an obsession with them to have this general captured alive.

Wen Tianxiang (文天祥) became my Chinese Sir Galahad. Galvanized by father's impressive dramatization—the picture of this imposing patriot, the pride of Chinese traditional history, naturally became my eternal love and role model as well. The child in me yearned to be him astride his steed at the head of the solid blocks of thousands of his followers. Father's flashing eyes and multifold character roles in the drama (which included a wide-ranging repertoire of sound effect) always held his audience in thrall.

One moment, father was the drummer whose heart-thudding drumbeats became as stirring as a full-blown tornado that churned through the army—a solid block of faceless humanity amidst glistening spears, lances and upraised swords afire in the relentless sun. Their inscrutable expressions belied the tumultuous rush of hot blood coursing through their veins. Next, father became the horses straining and pawing vigorously, stirring up a curtain of choking sand, intoxicated with the madness for action. Like squares of ripened corn rippling in the wind, the iron-clad army glistened and shimmered in the desert sun while the pennants bearing the formidable "WEN", surname of the General, flapped madly in the wind. All eyes were focussed on the majestic, silent figure on his horse, his proud horse hair plume flirting tantalizingly on his steel helmet.

When the stirring word "Charge!" thundered from the General, I, the child was blindly galloping at full speed as well, bravely, and with furious abandon into the dust storm stirred up by the human tide of my followers. The ground shivered and shook in the apocalyptic roar of pounding horses and charging men. Just as the millions of locusts that blocked out the sun, so the cloud of arrows from both armies turned day into night. In the dust storm of darkness, the ferocious armies clashed and crashed onto the quivering earth. The Heavens seemed to take sides—a human tornado churned and swirled in a mad frenzy— the eye of the fearful phenomenon was my hero. Father's vocal orchestra screeched to a crescendo and as suddenly it dipped into a dying echo . . . and . . . a dreadful silence. Just as the dark cloud of locusts had gone, revealing a bleak earth of the dead and twisted bare corn stalks; so too, with the dying breath of the battle, the earth was strewn with the dead and dying men among the twisted, bloodied lances and spears. The battle was over—the Mongol horde's cherished dream had materialized—they had captured the prized General alive. The privilege of this honour fell on Ogodei, the third son of the great Ghengis Khan.

The Mongols kept Wen in prison for four years using every inducement and bribe to get him to serve the Yuan Empire. The alternative was torture and death which he chose. Wen produced some literary works while in prison, one of which was "Song to my unbending spirit." Like Yue Fei, Wen Tianxiang's life-long dream was to keep China and Chinese civilisation safe from the barbarians. He had given his all—true to his Fatherland to the last. If only his enemies had known how this poem is sacrosanct to their prisoner-of-war, they would not have humbled themselves to lavish luxuries and indulgence on him during the three years:

> Ever since the beginning of time
> Can you tell me who never died?
> Then why not leave this pure heart of mine
> To complete forever with the blue of the sky?

So penned this literati who became the iconic general of traditional China.

As much as China admired patriotism, so naturally the most heinous of crimes was being a traitor to one's country. It didn't seem too long ago that the world had held traitors with the utmost of contempt. Beheading and quartering such specimen had been in practice. China had gone further—the heads of these reviled creatures were impaled in public as a mark of shame.

Wen Tianxiang too, was deified. Monuments and statues of him are scattered all over China. Wen's Ancestral Temple in Beijing has been well preserved, retaining the architectural style of the Ming Dynasty. True to the quotation from Wen's writing—

"All men are mortal, but my loyalty will illuminate the annals forever."

At this stage of the tale, the inspired child had instantly switched sides—I was relieved that I was not born a man who had to face the obligation to die for the country. It was not that bad, really, to be a "useless girl" after all!

Father's talent for teaching history and culture through story-telling was not unique at all. This form of oral transmission had been very popular in China for centuries; it had proven to be a very popular and successful means of reaching the semi-literate and illiterate population base. I had seen films and pictures of such story-tellers sitting by their little tables, with their eternal pots of tea, fanning themselves sedately while bringing to life the grandeur of the Beijing Opera to their enthralled audience.

These tea houses for "yum chah" and "dim sim" with such riveting entertainment had been an important conduit to the world of culture and history which had enriched only the educated classes in the past. "Yum chah" in the Cantonese dialect literally means "drink tea". "Dim sum" mistakenly spelt as "dim sim" literally means "a bit for the heart"—can be translated as "snack" (to satisfy) the heart and assuage the pangs of hunger.

The colourful make-up of the actors, their stunning costumes and headgear prevalent in the Ming Dynasty (1368-1644) lend an exotic splendour to the stage. It is the various colours of the heavily painted faces that symbolise the character and role of the actors—Red symbolises loyalty, integrity and bravery; while white would denote shrewdness and cunning.

*2 Stunning costumes and headgear signify status & authority.

The art of acting and gesticulation is highly stylised in keeping with the conventionalised and rigid pattern in singing, recitation and chanting. What adds to the thrilling excitement of the performance is that every gesticulation, expression and movement is synchronised with the music, heart-throbbing drumbeats and clashing cymbals.

The male personages in Beijing Operas fall under four general roles. Three of the male roles are shown here:

The sheng are male roles, subdivided into *"laosheng, xiaosheng* and *wusheng. Laosheng* are elderly or middle-aged men with beards. Those skilled in the martial arts come under the designation *wusheng."*

*3 Man threatened with sword, (without costume &
headgear) signifies loss of authority and status

The dan, the female roles are subdivided into six roles.
Their costumes and the colours of their faces would
define their station in life and the character they depict—
malicious, comic or unsophisticated.

*4 Postures and gesticulations are important in operas.

Our parents were married in the early years of the world's Great Depression and life must have been stressful for them when their children trooped into the world faithfully year by year. The birth of mother's first child must have been a frightening experience for her, due to the sudden leap from an uninformed cloistered life to the full responsibility of motherhood. Father had to employ a servant and a maid to help out in domestic demands and this had unfortunately eroded into the household expenses which resulted in our living on very basic food. Father had not been able to provide mother the traditional nutritious food needed by the nursing mother during the first month of the birth of a child. The Chinese believe that nutritious food should be specially prepared: such as food being fried in sesame oil, with wine and fresh ginger etc.

We had a happy childhood however; father, the baby-sitter in the evenings when he returned from work kept us happily occupied. We were always entertained by father's operatic performances and during the weekends, he even managed to make our calligraphy and writing lessons a fun session. Father must have missed the delight of live operas but managed to draw his cultural sustenance from the one and only one, cracked, long-playing vinyl record which coughed and screeched from an aged gramophone. He was in the prime of his life—a vibrant young man under whose protective wings he sheltered a young, energetic, trusting wife and a brood of bubbling, happy children. The only unhappy time we had to endure was having to swallow cod liver oil in the mornings and to drink sweet, condensed milk when we were unwell.

If life had been a struggle for our parents, mother never complained about it and father seemed to be in his element as provider and protector of his family. He was respected in society, loved at home and was fully aware of the responsibility demanded of him as a father and husband. Both our parents seemed to take the challenges they faced with optimistic resilience which seemed to iron out the bumps in the road ahead in this troubled period in history.

The sentiment so well-articulated by Professor Lin Yutang springs to mind:

> "There comes a time in our lives when the innocence of spring is a memory and the exuberance of summer a song whose echoes faintly remain in the air, when, as we look out on life, the problem is not how to grow but how to live truly, not how to strive and labour but how to enjoy the precious moments we have, not to squander our energy but how to conserve it in preparation for the coming winter . . ."[*5]

CHAPTER 6

THE SCHOLAR MANDARINS

F ather, as were all traditional Chinese, placed a great value on education since the educated class in China was revered in society. The best of the scholar-officials in the Mandarin class were esteemed as the Superior Man, the embodiment of all that is noble, virtuous and humane. These literati, steeped in the Confucian Classics, disciplined by a punishing regime of studies would be deemed fit to wear the mantle of responsibility and authority. It would be their duty to assist, (criticise, if the occasion demanded it) and advise the Emperor to transform and shape an orderly world.

In Ancient China, the Mandarins, the scholar-gentry class was on the top rung of the social hierarchy not only because of the Chinese respect for education but because to have one's son accepted into this hierarchy, the pride and glory would spread beyond the family to the entire village or clan AND people with the same surname as well. The scholars would have to go through punishing ordeals to get to the position of a Court Mandarin. This eminent scholar-gentry class comprised only 1.5% of the population at the beginning of the 19th Century. There were three tiers of stringent examinations; many aspirants would have fallen by the wayside, but for the clever and lucky chosen few, even to be successful in the first examination and emerge as the *"hsiu-t'sai"*—"Flowering Talent" would free him and his family from taxation for life and he himself would be exempt from any form of corporal punishment such as flogging. He would, however, not be qualified for service in the bureaucracy. The average age of these candidates were twenty-four. This first success would entitle him the honour to be paraded through the streets with colourful banners, beating of gongs and drums with the entire village basking in his glory.

Confucius' teaching emphasizes the doctrine of equality of education for all, but when it came to the Imperial Examination System which was a filtering system to cream off the most talented, this avenue was unfortunately not accessible to certain elements in society—some of those excluded from this Golden Gate to respectability, just to name a few—included actors, slaves, children of prostitutes, offspring of some menial employees of officialdom, policemen . . . Naturally, women had never been allowed any ticket of entry! The crème de la crème, chosen to govern the country would be seen as incarnation of the star god. He, the 君子 *"juunzi", the* "superior" man would be differentiated from the uneducated, the "inferior" or "small" man, the class to be governed.

Both Mencius, one of the most famous disciples of Confucius, and Hsun-tze, a cynical realist, believed that not all men are created equal. This is the Law of Nature— no two men of equal stations could command each other. If the social structure of an ant colony has adapted to this, we humans, who have a complex many-tiered hierarchy can be more than adaptive. So in the Confucian hierarchy there existed the Superior Man, the *"juunzii"*—the scholar who could "labour" with his mind; and the Lesser Man, he who couldn't labour with his mind, laboured with his hands—the peasant farmers and labourers.

The Imperial Examination System was introduced as early as the Han period (206.BC) reaching an impressive level of sophistication by the 11th Century. By the time of the Ming Dynasty (1368-1644) and the Qing (Ch'ing) Dynasty (1644-1911) this had represented a formidable ordeal. There were three formal examinations and a final test a scholar had to labour through to be admitted into the Hanlin Academy. "One needed the spiritual strength of a dragon-horse, the physique of a donkey, the insensitivity of a woodlouse, and the endurance of a camel" to go through these examinations."[1]

We follow the ordeal of Chiang Monlin facing the first Civil Examination which was being held in Shaoshing, in his district. Most candidates like Monlin had to travel on foot to their destination accompanied by a male servant carrying his luggage of clothes, books, writing materials and beddings, slung on two ends of a bamboo pole.

Roll call on this day held at the spacious court fronting the entrance of the Examination Hall started at four in the morning. A large crowd of literati, several thousand in number, each wearing a red tasselled hat and carrying a lighted lantern shivered through the chilly autumn morning. The dignified Prefect with his vermillion pen at his impressive desk called out and ticked off the name as the candidate stepped forward to be subjected to the routine of a thorough body search including his headgear. Written notes or texts were strictly prohibited in the examination hall.

The candidates then moved in a single file to their respective seats which were numbered. They were then handed the examination papers after the detachable slips of papers on which their names were written had been torn off. To avoid favouritism, the examination papers only bore a sealed number which was to be opened only after the papers had been marked and the successful candidates selected. Examination questions were promptly displayed to the candidates by means of cubic lanterns. Questions boldly written in black characters on the white screen lit by the candle of the lanterns were distinctly visible from a distance when the bearers paraded up and down the aisles.

At about the hour of noon, officials checked the progress of each candidate by stamping a red seal on the spot where the last character was written. The first call for the collection of examination scripts occurred at four in the afternoon preceded by the sound of roaring cannon. The gates were then flung open and the candidates filed out to the music of a performing band in view of the multitude of waiting families and relatives outside the gate. The gate clanged to an abrupt close with the exit of the last candidate. The second cannon roar for paper collection and ceremonious exit of candidates took place an hour later. The last call for collection occurring at six in the evening was a silent affair—no cannon, no music.

In the week or ten days' interim while waiting for the examination results, there was much to distract the anxiety of the candidates. Temporary restaurants with food and the famous Shaoshing wine at moderate prices blended well with the delightful entertainment by the travelling theatres. Others chose to stimulate their mind with playing chess at the numerous chess stands or browsing in the multitude of book stores. There was also opportunity for the nervous wrecks to squeeze in whatever time they could in the laborious task of committing the Classics to memory.

On the day that the results were to be publicised, the roar of the cannon with the striking of the band brought about a heavy surge of the waiting crowd—candidates and family members to the high spacious wall opposite the entrance of the Examination hall. The list of numbers of the successful candidates set down in a circular formation was pasted on the wall. This pattern was used to avoid the pitfall of finding one's identity at the bottom of the list.

The second session of the examination took place within a few days. This was another ordeal for many; it was anticipated that many candidates would be expected to be weeded out again. The last and final session was a mere perfunctory gesture by comparison—in addition to an essay, the candidates were expected to present a section of *The Imperial Instruction on Morals.* This was a rare treat to savour—the candidates were permitted to copy from the text they brought into the hall. The Supervisor on this occasion was the Imperial Examiner himself.

Early in the morning, some days later, Chiang Molin was awakened by a tom-tom outside his window. It was an official reporter who came to congratulate him on the award of the First Degree. The official announcement prominently written on a piece of red paper measuring six by four feet read as follows: "His Majesty's Imperial Vice-Minister of Rites and Concurrently Imperial Examiner of Public Instruction for the Province of Chekiang etc., wishes that your honourable person, Chiang Monlin, is awarded the Degree of Wu-shen *"Hsiu Tsái"* and entitled to enjoy the privilege of entering District Government School as a government scholar . . ."*2

The chief requirement for success in the Examinations lay in a thorough knowledge of the Confucian Classics—a commitment to memory of a prodigious amount of work; a thorough knowledge of historical literature and a mastery of several poetic styles. It was during the Southern Sung Dynasty, (1127-1279AD) that the prominent scholar-philosopher, Zhu Xi, selected four books from the Confucian Classics to be base texts for the Imperial Examination. These books known as Si Shu wielded great influence on traditional Chinese thinking. The candidates also had to write their papers in the notorious eight-legged essays which really required the mastery of a technical expertise and had been rightfully criticized for the sterility and formalization of the classical tradition. Confucian Classics were written in a ponderous, archaic language without punctuation and so esoteric in nature that it was beyond the comprehension of the common man. As early as the Northern Sung Dynasty (960-1126AD) the Prime Minister Wang An-Shih wrote: "What a student should learn are practical matters concerning the world and the nation."

If only that advice had been heeded! It was not an accident that China's scream for reform at the outset of the 20th Century demanded the abolishment of this ponderous Examination System—the catch-cry of the day was a concentration on Mathematics and Science. China had to reform to survive—the Confucian Literati became as effective as a museum antique.

Ponderous or not, the Chinese Civil Examination in principle had its value in history and traditional China had been shaped by it. The West had been sufficiently impressed by it as to adopt it for employment in their Government Service. The First Examination which produced the *"hsiu ts'ai"* (Flowering Talent) was normally held in the local city and the candidate would be required to sit for the examination again every three years to maintain his status should he fail to be accepted for the second tier of Examination.

This Second Examination to get the *"chu-jen"* degree, "Recommended Man" was held in the Provincial capital. The average age of the candidate would be around thirty. Only a tiny proportion, sometimes one in a hundred would venture to pass this examination. Again, much fan-fare would accompany the candidate who would have hoisted banners which read: "Candidates for the Imperially Decreed Provincial Examination" preceding his august being. To enjoy the glory of this new status, the aspiring candidate would have a vast, painful track to cover—literally, on foot. Very often, his family would have to endure deep impoverishment, even starvation, to get this favourite son to acquire this honour. Poems have been written of old mothers or wives sewing themselves blind, deep into the night, in order to provide the would-be scholar the necessary attire to keep him warm. He would have a servant to carry three long boards to furnish as shelf, desk and seat; carriers with baskets of food and water, bedding, clothes books and writing utensils.

Although getting this degree would not guarantee him anything further than a minor official position, it would enhance his prestige and improve his economic situation further. He, the "Recommended Man," would be elevated from his common status and be permitted to wear distinctive gowns and headgear.

To achieve a more senior career the "Recommended Man" would need to sit for the Metropolitan Examination to be held in the Capital a few months later. Here, the chances were that only one in thirty might succeed in acquiring the degree of "*jin shi*"—"Presented Scholar". The average age of the candidate would be around thirty-five. Success in this examination would be rewarded with nobility status. His distinctive gown and headgear would dignify him for appointment to middle rank official in the bureaucracy—possibly even a position in the palace. Provincial magistrates and important Assistant Secretarial posts would come from this noble class.

The ordeal did not stop here however, for he would have to sit for the final test, the Palace Examination to be presided over by the Emperor himself. This examination did not fail any of the candidates; the aim was to grade them in order of merit. The emperor's role was, in practice, assumed by individuals of high academic calibre, who, to reflect the sovereign's official responsibility would cast the questions in the style of an imperial pronouncement:

"I am the Son of Heaven, responsible for governing the Empire. Night and day I rack my brains so that the people will be able to live in tranquility. Fortunately I have this opportunity to pose questions to you graduates and I wish to hear your well-considered opinions on the following." There was also a standard formula for the answers: "I, Your humble servant, a superficial scholar newly advanced, not realizing where I was, have ventured to state my own views and am so ashamed of offending the Majesty of the Emperor that I do not know where to hide. I respectfully submit my answer."*3

The new *"jin shi"* were then rewarded with an official banquet and later attended a ceremony when they made obeisance towards the imperial residence to convey their gratitude. The next obligation was to attend a ceremony at the temple of Confucius. The top palace graduates would be admitted into the Hanlin Academy and would expect high offices after a period in the Imperial Secretariat. It would be quite a normal outcome for the Emperor to choose the top successful candidate as husband for one of his daughters. This would be the aspirant's wildest dream! Unfortunately, there had been stories and operas based on some ungrateful wretches who would abandon their wives and families to grasp this opportunity. Often these tear-jerkers would unfold a story of supreme sacrifices and deprivations endured by the wives and families in order to make it possible for them to participate in the examination.

One of the most popular Chinese operas is about Qing Xianliang, the abandoned wife of Chen Shimei, the heartless husband who was the top graduate of the Hanlin Academy (Song Dynasty 960-1126AD) and who became the Emperor's son-in-law. This abandoned first wife, Qing Xianliang, accompanied by her two children was free to seek him out after his parents had died of starvation. The agony of the long journey on foot could only be surpassed by the humiliation of having to kneel their way through the multitudes of court entrances. Chen Shimei in fear of his loss of new-found glory and punishment by the Emperor ordered one of his guards to murder his wife and children. On learning the truth, the guard saved their lives by committing suicide and Qing Xianliang finally found her way to see Bao Zeng, an upright minister in the Imperial Court. Facing the threat of the Princess and the Empress, Bao Zeng attempted the easy way out by offering Qing Xiangliang some silver to retract her accusation. When Qing Xiangliang threw away the silver in disgust, Bao Zeng inspired by her spirit and overcome with shame, risked his own life by ordering the execution of the royal son-in-law. Bao Zeng has gone down in history as the epitome of the principled Mandarin and court official.

The little girl enjoyed this opera immensely because father with his flamboyant flourishes would impersonate Bao Zeng with great gusto and authority. He could even produce a wide range of sound effects to bring to life a vibrant fanfare to announce the arrival of this august personage. The fascinated girl was particularly enchanted by father's impersonation of the different characters and particularly when he stroked the invisible, fearful long beard of Bao Zeng while strutting about the stage in his various moods.

The famous short story writer P'u Sung-ling (from *The Chinese Experience)* vividly described the ordeal in his account of the seven transformations of an examination candidate:

P'u Sung-ling described the ordeal starting from the first step the candidate took on his foot journey to the examination centre. His feeling was that of a beggar, weighed down by his heavy load of clothes and books, panting wearily to his destination. On arrival, he was treated like a prisoner having to undergo a thorough body search by the guards and being shouted at by the soldiers. Then, with outstretched neck peering out of his tiny cell, he resembled the larva of a bee. After completion of the examination, he would totter in a haze back to his cell, very much like a sick bird released from its cage. Waiting for the examination result would reduce him to a nervous wreck, so he was easily startled by the most familiar sounds; his restlessness was similar to that of a monkey on its leash. When he received news of his failure in the examination, he would collapse in a senseless heap, lying rolled onto his side, motionless like a poisoned fly. On returning to his senses, his cell would have the appearance of a tornado wreck—he had smashed and wrecked everything while cursing and swearing at the illiteracy of the examiners. At this stage, he was not unlike a pigeon among its smashed eggs.

There was a story of a downtrodden peasant who, after years of failure in the Imperial Examinations went berserk on receiving the news of his success at last. His bully of a father-in-law, who was a butcher, slapped him on the cheek to bring him to his senses when it suddenly dawned on him that the pain in his hand was inflicted by the spirits in punishment for his audacity to slap an "immortal".

The ultimate aim of the scholars was to get into the Hanlin academy and be conferred the honour of an Imperial appointment. Many never reached this far—and these were given positions such as minor magistrates, teachers or governors of minor provinces. I remember father's pompous observation that any failed Hanlin scholar would have earned his esteemed position in society. Sycophants would even believe that the scholar's farts were fragrant.

Many of these under-achieved scholars would resort to selling their calligraphy, painting or poetry. Calligraphy and Chinese brush painting are closely intertwined; a good painter needs to be a keen and good calligraphist. The greatest calligraphist, Wang Xizhi, defined his art in the following terms:

"Every horizontal stroke is like a mass of clouds in battle formation, every hook like a bent bow of the greatest strength, every dot like a falling rock from a high peak, every turning of the stroke like a brass hook, every drawn-out line like a dry vine of great old age, and every swift and free stroke like a runner on the start."[*4]

The Chinese value calligraphy purely for the aesthetic nature of its strokes and grouping of lines. Each line or dot is executed with a single stroke of the brush which cannot be corrected or touched up. The aesthetic quality is the result of cooperation between the mind and the hand. Every single stroke in good calligraphy gives the sensuous pleasure of being akin to nature; it has the energy of a living thing. Every light or heavy sweep of the brush, every straight or curved stroke, every dot and dash breathes with life in its spontaneity of execution. Its very simplification of presentation and suggestive effect gives a thrill of aesthetic pleasure as of being in direct contact with nature. Chinese paintings since the Sung period (960-1276 AD) would often include calligraphy in the form of a poem or inscription. This often aids to enhance the meaning and appreciation of the painting.

The exquisite beauty of Chang Yee's painting—The Happiness of the Fish—is heightened by his calligraphy inscription of the following philosophical discourse from the text, *Chuang Tzu*:

Two Daoist philosophers, Chuang Tzu and Hui Tzu were enjoying themselves on the bridge over the River Hao. Chuang Tzu happened to remark that the graceful swimming of the fish seemed to express their happiness.

"'Those little fish swimming hither and thither are very graceful' remarked Chuang Tzu, 'they are expressing their happiness.'

'You are not a fish,' answered Hui Tzu, 'how can you know that the fish are happy?'

'You are not me,' rebuked Chuang Tzu, 'how can you know that I do not know the happiness of the fish?'

'Well, I am not you, I naturally don't know your feeling,' resumed Hui Tzu. 'But obviously you are not a fish and it is plain that you cannot know the happiness of these fish.'

'Please let's go back to where we began,' said Chuang Tzu. 'Your question of how I know the happiness of the fish shows that you already realize that I do know the happiness of the fish. I know it here, above the River Hao, on this bridge."*5

I am indebted to my father for his calligraphy lessons to his children. I, unfortunately, did not have a formal Chinese education; but the sentient pleasure I derive from Chinese calligraphy and brush painting is an invaluable gift. Just as a little tortoise would shrink its head into its shell and tensed itself to immobility, the little girl would tense up hoping to deflect any punishing pronouncement as: "That stroke (or that dot) is not strong enough . . ." The painful regime would start with practice and more practice till the effort would graduate to: "Yes, a little improvement . . ." The condescending remark was small comfort, but an earned comfort and it was pleasurable. Father had the gift of bringing about a happy humming activity in his children's class. It is a sad pity that I have to rely on sketchy memories of my family in the other world, the other life. Cyclone Tracy that flattened Darwin in 1974 had not forgotten me—she had seen to all my treasured records including my collection of brush paintings on silk scrolls and has curtained off that other world in a thick mist.

Life for many a successful scholar who became important Court Ministers had their stories of stress and frustration. Court intrigues and corruption had driven the noble and virtuous to abandon themselves to nature and lived a life of poverty. Albeit, Chinese history has many proud sons and daughters on its record. Heroes such as the revered Bao Zeng and the innumerable patriots who had sacrificed their lives for the country were elevated to deity status. Temples in honour of them are tourist sites in today's China. Another great military hero honoured through the ages was Kongming. A temple in his honour is in Sichuan today. Kongming has been credited with many famous exploits. The most popular one is this cheeky "Kongming borrowed some arrows" from *The Romance of the Three Kingdoms,* Volume 1.

Kongming, also known as Zhuge Liang (181-234 AD), was a learned scholar and intellectual in the period of The Three Kingdoms. His fame as a military strategist has earned him the nickname of the "Crouching Dragon".

Chou Yu, his Commander-in-Chief was jealous of his popularity. He therefore decided to set him a task which he believed would be impossible for him to accomplish. He ordered him to deliver 100,000 arrows within ten days so as to defend themselves from their enemy's impending attack. It was no secret to Kongming that his Commander-in-Chief had plans to destroy him. So when Kongming was given the order by Chou Yu, he graciously informed him that ten days would be too late to save themselves from the enemy. He suggested that the arrows should be ready within three days and he would immediately get to work as soon as he received the required boats and materials from his Commander-in-Chief.

As anticipated, Kongming was not surprised when he witnessed the delight of the Commander-in-Chief who took the golden opportunity to remind him that he would lose his head should he fail to deliver the arrows within the prescribed time. The elated Chou Yu drank with his friend to celebrate the good news and informed him that he would be looking forward to the happy day to receive Kongming's head on a platter. He would ensure that to happen by ordering his men to delay delivery of the boats and materials requested by Kongming.

Kongming in anticipation of this had requested Lu Su, his friend, to lend him a score of vessels each manned by thirty men. The vessels were furnished with blue cotton screens and had bundles of straws lashed to the sides of the boats. His friend was most perplexed that Kongming did nothing towards making any arrows beyond this preparation. It was in the early hours of the third morning that Kongming ordered the twenty boats which were fastened together by robes to sail right into the heavy fog towards the enemy's camp by the river. All the boats were soon lined up in a single line, with prows facing west by the enemy's camp.

Everything was in a hushed silence except for Kongming's happy gulping of wine with his friend. Then, by the early hour of the morning, Kongming ordered his men to beat the drums and to shout as loudly as they could to add to the infernal din. The shocked enemies believing that an ambush by their enemies was upon them immediately had all the archers and crossbow men lined along the beach and shot into the fog. The arrows from a legion of more men fell thick like rain. Knowing that the enemies would not risk charging towards them in the fog, Kongming had the boats turned around so that the prows pointed eastwards till both sides of the boats were soon bristling with arrows. The drumbeats and the shouting continued till the sun was high and the fog had dispersed. As the boats sailed downstream, the crew cried derisively: "Thank you for the arrows, Minister!"

Kongming remarked to his companion that since each boat would have collected about five to six thousand arrows, he had exceeded the required number of arrows. He cheerfully reminded his men that all the borrowed arrows would be shot back to the enemies the next day.

When Chou Yu congratulated his general, he grudgingly admitted that Kongming's superhuman predictions compelled his esteem. Kongming tossed it off that there was nothing remarkable in that trifling trick; that he had studied the "elements" and expected the night to be foggy.

Chou Yu sighed sadly in admitting that Kongming was indeed admirable:

> Thick lies the fog on the river,
>   Nature is shrouded in white,
> Distant and near are confounded,
>   Banks are no longer in sight.
> Fast fly the pattering arrows,
>   Stick in the boats of the fleet,
> Now can full tale be delivered,
>   Kongming is victor complete.*[6]

CHAPTER 7

NO MORE "AH QS"

"We shall teach such a lesson to these perfidious hoards that the name of European will hereafter be a passport of fear . . . ."

So ran the extract from *The Times of London* during the period of the Opium Wars in the 1840s.[*1]

My father was born in 1895 in the town of Chaozhou, in Guangdong Province, Southern China. He was the eldest of three children and his extended family of eight included his first wife and two daughters. Japanese incursions into Chinese territory and the invasion of Manchuria in 1931 had been causing turmoil and widespread starvation. Father was forced to leave his family in search of salvation for those he left behind and joined the exodus of Chinese migrants across the oceans. The diaspora of Chinese seeking a better life elsewhere was nothing new in Chinese History. This scenario became acute in China's darkest hour—after the Opium Wars. Father could be considered one of the "lucky" ones compared to the unfortunate thousands known as "the pigs" of an earlier period. The infamous "Trade of pigs", compliment of Great Britain, occurred after the two Opium Wars (1840-1850s). The term "shanghaied" which graced the English dictionary was never more busy than this sad time in history when thousands of coolies had been kidnapped and tricked into slavery overseas.

The early Americans were not the only people, therefore, who lived off the blood of slaves. The victorious British were among other European nations which kidnapped and drugged hundreds of Chinese coolies (labourers) before throwing them into filthy, crowded ships for slave labour in their colonies. There was a high mortality rate, an average of half of the passengers perished during the voyages. All this happened despite the fact that Britain had attempted to abolish the slave trade as early as 1807. There were, however, many Britons who suffered from a guilty conscience. One such was John Bowring, the British Consul in Canton who wrote to the Foreign Secretary, Lord Malmesbury in 1852:

". . . . iniquities scarcely exceeded those practised on the African middle passage have not been wanting . . . the jails of China (have been) emptied to supply "labour" to British Colonies . . . hundreds (of coolies) gathered together in (holding pens) stripped naked, and stamped or painted with the letter C (California), P (Peru) or S (Sandwich Islands) on their breasts, according to destination."[*2]

Chinese emigrants like my father, were scattered all over the world. In the era of the "Gold Rush" many emigrants had rushed to the "Golden Mountain" (San Francisco, USA) where the streets of the city were purported to be paved with gold! By 1849, there were 90,000 gold-diggers in this city, the gateway to the Californian goldfields. Others had emigrated to Australia for the same purpose— to dig for gold. "Dinkum", "real gold" in Cantonese would have set them and their families up for life. Dinkum was indeed, a very enticing beacon. Father, however, happened to find his way to Malaya through the Chinese "network" of using the "credit-ticket system". One had to pay for the voyage in unmitigated labour—ten hours a day, seven days a week to whatever business one was contracted to. I have no recollection of how many years it took father to discharge his debt nor what percentage of his wages he was able to send home to his family.

"Life in this draconian "servitude" had been taxing, very draining . . ." father recalled, a hint of a thin mist veiled his far-away look as his voice trailed away. There was no such thing as Leave of any shape or kind; not even sick leave. I remember his narrating how he had to sleep on a mat in a warehouse among crates of goods and how he nearly died from tetanus when a rusty nail went through his foot. He had been bed-ridden and on an enforced fast for about thirty-six hours. Food had been mass-cooked for the employees who were over-worked and hungry. It was not from a lack of charity that father had to limp his painful way to the dining area for his meals. One had to look after number one of course—every over-worked employee with his nose in the trough had barely time to take a deep breath. There had never been enough food for all.

"Overseas Chinese" could always get assistance from some benevolent association or club based on dialect or surname groups where one could find means to survive. It was a marvel to us that father, with barely "three years and eight months of formal education" (as alleged by him), could have acquitted himself so well as to emerge an accepted "leader" and "elder" in the society of his time. He must have been an avid reader under some wise guidance. Father had been an intellectual in his day and used to read profusely as far as I can remember. He smelt of antiquated Confucian texts and his right thumb and index finger seemed to be never still, even when he was relaxing. Both fingers were always busy in a continuous choreography of dances—father was always practising writing invisible Chinese calligraphy. The formation of each Chinese character has to be learnt by heart—a dot in the wrong place of a character can alter its meaning drastically. Father's popularity as a public speaker stemmed from the fact that he could keep his listeners captivated and amused. It was not very amusing for him when the Japanese decided to pay our village a visit to purge our village of "jungle rats"—Chinese underground freedom fighters. Father's eloquence landed him in a Japanese prison camp.

The Japanese invasion of Malaya (8-12-1941) was noted for its ruthless mass slaughter of the Chinese. The subjugated Malayans had to bow to every Japanese soldier on sight. On Japanese days of celebration, it was mandatory for Malayans to attend en mass and shout "BANZAI!" three times while punching the air with the right arm in a triumphant shout of jubilation. Its literal meaning is "10,000 years" (of life), equivalent to our "God save the King!" Father, as with most Chinese would take the opportunity to shout as lustily as they could "BANGSAI!" In the Hokkien and Teochew dialects, this word means "SHIT".

We children were always entertained by father's rich repertoire of stories of glory and valour from Chinese myths and history. He also had a rich treasure of jokes and sarcasm. I can still see him patting the tell-tale bulge of his belly with operatic satisfaction as he regaled us with the tale of the starving beggar. An abject beggar had been hauled to court by a fat restaurateur who objected to his inhaling the fragrance of scrumptious food emerging from his kitchen window. He wanted the beggar to pay for this privilege! The magistrate called for some silver coins and had them jingled in a container. He then coolly dismissed the case—the restaurateur had been duly paid—didn't he hear the sound of the jingling coins?

Father's sarcasm could be biting as well as entertaining. When his anger was aroused, he would resort to this weapon for attack. On one occasion when father was very angry with one of my brothers over some lazy and stupid behaviour, father complimented him by saying that my brother reminded him of the story of "*Ah Soh*". (The name means "Ah Stupid") Ah Soh was a mean thief because he was too lazy to work for a living. Once he stole two ounces of silver and hid them behind a brick in the wall of his house. To safeguard his loot, he wrote: "Ah Soh did not hide his silver here."

Still licking his wounds from the world of humiliation after the Opium Wars, whose door had only just been closed behind him, father must have been suffering from some form of disorientation on the threshold of the new, alien world in which he found himself. The dying spasm of a proud empire had turned the Chinese world upside down and father was still "in mourning," as were many other traditionalist Chinese of his day. He valued the glory of the golden past—surely, the pride of the Celestial Empire could still be salvaged to shape a new China? He taught his children that one should retain the best of one's culture and tradition which enhances one's morality and humanness; and that we could learn from our past to be resilient in the face of adversity. Chinese history and civilization therefore, became an important subject in our home-education syllabus and this was taught through stories and historical references.

Father's recent historical experiences had been challenging, courageous, sad and inspiring. Like many young students of his time, father too, was soon embroiled in the whirlpool of action in those heady days of mass discontent and rebellions. He was a young firebrand among other intellectuals swept along the tidal wave of hysterical demands to topple the Monarchy. The aftermath of the Opium Wars heralded an era of frenetic push for reforms and change in China—an ants' nest had been disturbed, thousands upon thousands of ants were rushing about in all directions biting and clamouring over writhing bodies . . .

The birth of the twentieth century in China had been one of prolonged labour of pain and anguish. The Western powers had subjected the Celestial Empire to abject humiliation . . . . China had been carved up for grabs—she seemed to belong to everyone who cared to drop by for a share of the pie. Suddenly the need for a total Cultural, Economic and Political spring-cleaning was considered to be of paramount importance. During the decade of 1900, reformer after reformer had one common ideology (very well and powerfully enunciated in an inflammatory tract in 1903) calling for the creation of a revolutionary army. It was imperative that China had to cleanse herself of the shame of 260 years of Manchu oppression and cruelty. It was time for "the sacred Han race, descendants of the Yellow Emperor" to reinstate their heritage and right— China had been under Manchu rule from 1644 to 1911.

"Remember! You are a Han Chinese! We Chinese have a proud and rich culture!" Father shook his fist and scowled at poor little me who tried to look as "Han" as possible whatever that might mean.

The "IN" things then were: Nationalism, Patriotism, Democracy, Progress and Freedom. To be thrown OUT were: Feudalism, Imperialism and Blind Adherence to Tradition. The clumsy, outmoded stranglehold of Confucian teaching, which favoured "the way of the Sages", instrumental in the discouragement of development of people's capabilities had to be tossed out! This rote-learning and copycat syndrome was seen as producing "mental cripples."

What an intellectual 180-degree turnaround against tradition! The privileged Confucian Civil Examination system had failed them. The classics of the past did not save them. Suddenly, China seemed to have woken up to a new dawn—and with one voice, the youth of the day were marching to the same drumbeat. The strident clashing of the cymbals was deafening, pre-empting that the road to a Modern China was to be littered with the corpses of an antique past. A clean broom was needed to sweep out the old. First and foremost, the education system had to undergo a radical change—Mathematics and the Sciences were the IN things. The clarion call was "LEARN FROM THE WEST!"

Father's eyes blazed fiercely when he told his children how the firebrand of the day strove to build a New China. China was boiling! Rage! Rage! Rage! As if on cue, onto the stage in the very first decade of the turbulent period of twentieth century China, stormed an influx of actors of a very diverse mix of elites and intellectuals many of whom had had the privilege of a Western education. Reformists, Revolutionists, all had one mindset—Change! Change! Reform! China must reform in order to survive.

In keeping with the need to purge out the old and instal the new for China's survival, the acclaimed Father of Modern China was the very antithesis of the traditional Confucian literati. Dr Sun Zhongshan was a Western-educated medical doctor and a Christian convert. Moreover, like all other reformers of the day, Dr Sun not only had cut off his pigtail in 1896, he had donned Western attire as well. Sun Zhongshan (1866-1925) had lived in Hawaii from the age of thirteen with his brother and uncle. He was educated in the USA where two of his uncles had emigrated in the Gold Rush days. He founded the "hundred-member chapter" of the Revive China Society in Hawaii and set up a similar group in Hong Kong.

I remember father's eyes ablaze with patriotic zeal when he instructed his children to bow to a photograph of a youngish, handsome mustached man in Western coat and tie. "Dr Sun Zhongshan," father would mutter with grave reverence as he doubled himself in a bow.

Our father? Another father? Father's father? This was most confusing to little me at that time. I had difficulty distinguishing Dr Sun from that other photograph of father's father high up on the wall above the family altar. That photograph of a benign spectacled old man with a wispy white beard and two perplexed little eyes peering from behind little round Gandhi glasses had always been an object of awed curiosity to me. The genteel old man in the half portrait was in an elegant brocade gown complemented with a soft brocade cap which I was convinced was actually a half watermelon. He too, was my father's father and I had wondered how many more fathers this poor soul had to kowtow to.

*3 Dr. Sun Zhongshan

As if this was not enough exercise for a little girl, next to the bespectacled melon-headed grandfather was a half portrait of our grandmother to whom kowtows were also due. She seemed to be warmly clothed in something suffocatingly tight and bore a remarkable resemblance to a well-trussed Italian sopressa salami. It was the face that fascinated me most—I knew that my teacher would have made me write a hundred lines "I must not be rude" had I made my thoughts known. I could not help wondering if the pencil-thin slits of her eyes in spite of a fixed pursed-lip smile were a grimace of pain caused by suffocation. Only later were we told that she was blind.

On Republic Day we would line up with father in front of Dr Sun's portrait and with a reverent kowtow, father would sing in a rich sonorous voice the National Chinese Anthem. This anthem spelt out Dr Sun's Three Principles which are entrenched as the ideology of the Chinese Nationalist Party. They are: Nationalism, (anti-Imperialism); Democracy (anti-Monarchy); and People's Livelihood (equated with Socialism).

We were quite happy to perform this ritual. He could have been meaner and made us kneel to kowtow not once, but three times, as we had to do on the death anniversaries of our grandfather and grandmother.

In the incendiary period of his young adulthood, father had bellowed that the time was ripe for change. Many of the Young Turks of the day, inspired and fortified by a Western Education gained overseas, believed passionately that they could "save China". They had a glimpse of the New World—a world of freedom and salvation for China through the treasure-house of literature which had highlighted China's failure. China had to come out of the Dark Ages and at once! Intellectuals and students soaked up whatever was modern and new, especially in economics and social matters.

The life-giving tonic was translations of works which included:

Adam Smith's *The Wealth of the Nations* (1900),
Herbert Spencer's *The Study of Sociology* (1903)
J.S. Mill's *On Liberty* (1903)
Huxley's *Evolution and Ethics* (1895),
Montesquieu's *The Spirit of Laws* (1909).

Visiting intellectuals from the West gave that needed extra boost—

John Dewey (1919-1921),
Bertrand Russell (1920-1921),
Albert Einstein (1922),
Bernard Shaw (1933)

Along with other publications, the magazine, *New Youth* (first published in 1915) had been a powerful catalyst in the tumultuous wind of change. Its founder was Chen Duxu who was then Dean of Letters at Beijing University. Chen had studied in Japan and northern France and with Hu Shi, another luminary, had been a zealous advocate of individual freedom. They were a formidable force in the New Culture Movement.

Communist Russia had been a timely inspiration. Marxism, Lenin and Trotsky were the stars that lit the way in China's hour of need. Li Dazhao the librarian at Beijing University wrote an introduction to Marxist theory, explaining such concepts as class struggle and Capitalist exploitation which was published in the May 1919 issue. Big Brother of the West helped to stoke the fire and lent a willing hand in the practical organization of Communist cells in China.

The person in power at this crucial time in history was Cixi, the Empress Dowager. There was some controversy over her reputation. One school of thought upheld her as an astute politician while another resented her Machiavellian talent in keeping power to herself at all costs. Cixi, under mounting pressure, had no choice but to announce a plan to phase in the Constitutional Principles in the New China over a nine-year tutelage period. Swept in the ferment of reform, the twenty-three-year-old Emperor Guangxu (a nephew of the Dowager) became the self-appointed head of the Reformists with edict after edict ordering reforms and drastic changes, especially in the areas of Commerce, Government, Education and the Military. But alas! That odious old toad, the Empress Dowager, fearful of having Manchu power and her own position undermined, locked up the Emperor and executed any reformers that she could lay hands on. So perished the ambitious Hundred Days' Reform.

Cixi had been the favourite concubine of the Emperor Xianfeng who died in 1861. From this time to her own death in 1908, Cixi had one aim in life—to have power firmly grasped in her hand. She succeeded in this for forty-seven years by appointing herself as Regent to a succession of infant emperors. On the eve of her own death, she appointed Puyi, the infant nephew of the Emperor Guangxu, to become the last Emperor of China. Poor little Puyi! He had never wanted to be Emperor. All he wanted was to be trained as a teacher in Britain—so averred his brother-in-law.

*4 Cixi, the Empress Dowager

Many "dark tales" have percolated through time about this powerful Dowager. Court intrigues and the suspicious death of the Emperor Guangxu as well as the demise of those who had displeased her, helped fuel the rumours. Cixi was often depicted as a ruthless, ambitious and sexually depraved tyrant. Her place in history has provided ample nourishment for the imagination of succeeding generations of Chinese. Local Chinese tourists to the Forbidden City used to find a stone well by the Palace of Peace and Longevity a fascinating object for photographs. The story went that when European troops surged into Beijing in 1900, the Empress Dowager summoned the Emperor Guangxu and his favourite concubine, Zhen Fei, to evacuate the Palace. The so-called Pearl Concubine begged that the Emperor be given permission to stay behind to negotiate with the invaders. The enraged Dowager promptly ordered that the recalcitrant be thrown into the well. An alternative version, however, offered by the Dowager's great, great nephew, a Manchu nobleman, was—yes, the Dowager did have a sharp tongue; but then, Zhen Fei had obligingly jumped into the well on th august lady's suggestion that she should do so to avoid the disgrace of being raped by the invaders.

In 1910, the brilliant Halley's Comet appeared and this was interpreted as an omen for great change. Moreover, natural disasters such as the outbreak of the pneumonic plague and the widespread rice famine as a result of the Yangtze breaking its banks helped to spell the end of Manchu rule—The Manchu Dynasty had lost "its mandate to rule."

Among the Reformers, one of the most prominent was Kang Yu-Wei, who argued that there was a place for Confucianism in the New China. Kang argued that Confucius, far from being a rigid conserver of the values of the past, was a creative, ethical leader and statesman and would be a relevant inspiration and source of guidance to the Reformers. An eminent scholar in history and the classics, Kang argued that many of the old, revered classics had been tampered with by Wang Mang and his Chief Minister to sanction the political and social programme of the day. Wang Mang, the "usurper" to the throne was the founder of the Xin Dynasty (9-23AD)

A belated reform of the government, army and navy was instituted in 1903. The building of a network of railway lines was also seen as of paramount importance. The out-moded Traditional Civil Service Examinations were abolished in 1905. The hitherto revered Confucian literati became an antiquated breed overnight.

One of the most brilliant writers and commentators in these heady days was Lu Xun (1881-1936) who was the first to venture into using the vernacular in his writing. Father led us into *"The True Story of Ah Q"* one of Lu Xun's powerful, amusing and bitingly sarcastic stories.

"Ah Q" (queue, pigtail), epitomized the subjugated Chinaman of the day—one of the milling social flotsam, a despicable, harmless odd-jobber, a product of the Opium Wars who accepted bullying and humiliation as a matter of course. Always resilient to press ahead, but too cowardly and self-deceiving, he resorted to claiming his moral superiority. Ah Q "has become the emblem of the seamier traditional national traits: self-delusion, defeatism, submission to force and authority, and boldness in browbeating the weak and helpless." This born loser came to a sorry and pathetic end of course—he was executed by a representative of the revolution for a robbery he had never committed, simply because he had been too cowardly to go through with it. Too late for him to wish that he should have had the guts to commit the crime.*5

With wrathful pride, father was adamant that China should no longer be known for her Ah Qs anymore! Little me applauded with lusty gusto! Too right! All "Qs" were a blooming nuisance! The little girl sighed in happy relief that she did not have to have a swishing pigtail as many little girls did. Didn't father himself admit that his pigtail had caused him frustration and embarrassment? It had often been dipped in the ink pot of the student who sat behind him in school? The back of his shirt became a canvas for abstract art, thanks to his swishing pig-tail. Little me had three good reasons to argue her case should that be necessary. These were:

1. The little girl was happy to keep her page-boy hair-cut which had earned her many scrumptious bribes when the time came for a hair-cut in the early days. She had enjoyed in particular a candy, a gorgeous red in colour, rather similar to Turkish Delight which had the magic power of stopping her howling the instant it was pushed into the open cavern of her mouth.

2. The little girl was happy that at the mature age of six, a hair-cut by the barber was something to look forward. She could recall the first time she went for a haircut at the barber shop and the humiliating deflation that consumed her when she boasted to her father that the Indian barber, (the one with a white dot between his eye-brows) had proposed marriage to her. She had expected her father to erupt into a thundering fury and storm into the shop to tweak the barber's ear for casting aspersions on his chaste daughter. Now in the full flush of maturity, she had accepted the fact that the course of true love is always tinged with bitterness and sweetness. The

bitterness was past and gone; the sweetness was the warm glow that she had a boyfriend!
3. The pigtail would endanger her life in time of war. The horrid boys in the back alleyways and parks were her sworn enemies. How DARE they exclude her from their games?

With dramatic aplomb, father narrated how he too, had risen to the occasion to do his bit for his people and his country. (At this point, the little girl felt that she could hear the triumphant clash of cymbals). So, along with the human wave of protesters, father queue-less, had his own soap box and shouted himself hoarse to arouse and cajole the ever-willing audience to wake up to reality.

May 4th 1919 saw the famous May 4th Movement when students all over the country stood up to the government of the day. The Movement had been triggered by news of how the Versailles Peace Conference was handling the situation of Shandong—Japan had laid claim to German rights in Shandong in 1914 and the powers of the day had decided in favour of the claim, a reward to Japan for being an ally of Britain and France in the First World War— obviously a back-room wheeling-and-dealing affair.

China, inspired by President Wilson's stress on national self-determination, had pinned her hope on Democracy and Justice. The ensuing disillusionment strangled China in a stultifying grip of disbelief. The betrayal had been more hurtful since China too had contributed to the war effort for the Allies—170,000 Chinese had the gruesome task of digging trenches to salvage corpses in the war zones in France. "Self-reliance!" thundered father. China was friendless! Then the floodgate swung open—three thousand students converged on Beijing Tiananmen Square in a demonstration. They had screamed and shouted; they had door-knocked with running appeals to the public, whose sympathy and support they seemed to have won. Public stands with free food and drink had been set up for the protesters, thousands of banners and cards had been contributed, money had been freely donated. The government had to cave in to the demented horde—China refused to sign the Treaty of Versailles. This moral victory set the tone for the cultural politics of the day.

Fresh from the cultural upheavals in China, we had an earful from father about the iniquity of opium; its perniciousness could be surpassed only by that of the poisonous red-haired barbarians, of which the worst were the British! They had poisoned the whole country! The Western colonial powers had squeezed China dry! Father's thundering voice shook the room. The resulting Opium Wars against the dumping of opium into China had crushed the empire, the once arrogant Celestial Empire was on her knees. Ringing in the ears of father and the Young Turks of his day was this strident threat from Lord Elgin, the British Plenipotentiary to China at this time:

> "Twenty four determined men with revolvers, and a sufficient number of cartridges, might walk China from one end to another."[*6]

This scornful assertion proved to be not too far-fetched. China had limited antiquated weapons to withstand the great maritime power of Britain.

Xenophobic China had this superior attitude about the Middle Kingdom from ancient times. "China Proper", the domain of the Han Chinese in the region of the Yellow River had always regarded inhabitants of the outer regions of Asia as barbarians; hence, the Great Wall of China had been built to shut them out. This racist attitude had been more pronounced with regard to non-Asian races.

The Middle Kingdom had historically seen itself as independent and self-sufficient and had nursed a haughty attitude towards non-Chinese people. A closed-door policy had been its historical practice. Marco Polo, like many Westerners of his time had been fascinated by the exotic "Cathay"—China. China's vulnerable exposure to the world came as a result of the British gung-ho determination to force trade in opium upon China in the 18th century. The British persistence in the China Trade arose from the fact that Britain, from 1664 onwards, had become dependent on tea from China which resulted in an imbalance of payment with China which demanded payment in Spanish silver dollars. The solution to this lay in forcing the British colony of India to grow opium which they had foisted upon China.

The Chinese Government had been against this trade in "poison" from the outset. The first of the three British trade missions to China was in 1797, led by Lord Macartney who had to endure haughty and humiliating treatment by the Chinese. This was not unexpected—there had been fifteen missions in the past—attempts by Portugal, the Netherlands, Russia and France had all failed.

The only port that foreigners had been permitted a limited foothold was in Canton in South China, (present-day Guangzhou). When the first mission arrived, the Chinese regarded it as a tribute mission. A large sign attached to the mast of the Ambassador's ship in big Chinese characters read: "Tribute from the Red Barbarians."

Compliments about each respective race flew freely. The label "red-haired barbarians" on the British had its origin in Sir Robert Napier, the first British Chief Superintendent of Trade in China. The choice of Napier was unfortunate—he was tall, ungainly, had red hair and a contemptuous regard of the Chinese. Napier wrote to Lord Grey: "The Chinese people wallow in the extreme degree of mental imbecility and moral degradation, dreaming themselves to be the only people on earth, and being entirely ignorant of the theory and practice of international law."*[7]

Napier was not aware that the Chinese Europeans were associated with were mainly the down-trodden coolies and servants. It was almost impossible for a Westerner, to go beyond this barrier during that period in history.

China's response to this unwelcome trade was to send Lin Zexu, the Governor of Hubei and Honan, a formidable mandarin of impeccable ability and reputation to stop the opium trade. The British Superintendent of Trade had to hand in the opium to Lin. 20,000 chests of opium were burnt in the presence of the British. The news outraged Britain. Commercial interests pushed strenuously for war with China to enforce the trade in opium. The Union Jack had been waved as vigorously as the cries for revenge had been deafening. The most powerful independent trading company, Jardine, Matheson and Company brayed the loudest war cry and volunteered to send more ships and military aid towards the war effort.

War was inevitable and in the face of British superior military might, China suffered a resounding defeat in the first Opium War in 1840. The First Peace Treaty forced on China resulted in the forced opening of Canton and the ceding of Hong Kong in perpetuity. To add insult to injury, China had to cough up six million silver dollars in indemnity—payment for extra expenses in the war.

Mandarin Lin Zexu, the Mandarin held responsible for the Opium Wars was sent in chains to face his punishment by the Emperor. He was exiled from China. Scores of Mandarins committed suicide in humiliation. Another war followed. By 1841, Britain had occupied several coastal cities in China and by the time of the Treaty of Nanking (Nanjing) 1840, concluded at gunpoint, the indemnity was raised to twenty-one million silver dollars.

By the end of the century, more treaty ports were forced opened and leased in perpetuity to foreign powers. Other Western powers also were racing to partake of this feast. Further concessions included consular rights and "the most favoured nation" clause gave the British the automatic right to any privilege that China extended to other powers. The Opium Trade was legalised in 1860.

R.B. Ebrey (Cambridge Illustrated *History of China*) affirmed that in 1729, only 200 chests of opium were sold in China. This figure jumped to 1,000 chests in 1767 and 4,500 chests by 1800. During the next quarter century, imports escalated to 10,000 chests and by the time of the first Opium War in 1839, the import figure rose to 40,000 chests.

In 1888, *The Times of London* estimated 70% of adult males in China were addicted to opium.

From the Emperor down to the abject derelict in the back alley, the stupor of opium fume had brought about a national paralysis. The Empress Dowager luxuriated in opiate oblivion while China burned.

The British firm Jardine, Matheson and Company which made its fortune from the Opium Trade with China took the trouble to issue a press release in 1858. It reassured the public that the sale of opium to China was for the benefit and comfort of the diligent Chinese.

There were, however, some conscience-stricken individuals in Britain. William Gladstone in 1842 had this to say:

> "I am in dread of judgement of God upon England for our national iniquity towards China."*8

The Treaty of Versailles was the match to the gunpowder keg. The humiliating stink of the Opium Wars must be eradicated once and for all. Father's rapid nodding of the head was in danger of causing it to drop off.

It was hoped that the New State and New Society of a modernized China that father and his ardent compatriots had fought for, should first of all, aim for China to be on an equal footing with the rest of the world. But— alas! much more blood had yet to flow—first from Japanese aggression and then from the struggle between Chiang Kaishek's Chinese Nationalist Party and Mao's Communist Party. It was not surprising to witness the mass hysteria that flooded the country when Mao declared in 1949 that China could stand up again at last. Would there be no more bloodbaths? Poor country! More disillusion, more blood to flow and now in the new millennium with the auspicious big-bang opening of the 2008 Beijing Olympics, China seems to be standing on her own feet again. Today she is a vociferous economic giant—China is in a hurry to catch up with the developed countries.

I wonder what would be father's reaction to today's China. Has her progress surpassed his wildest dreams? What was the Olympics slogan again? One World! One Dream! To many of the millions of Chinese caught in the time-warp of the remote countryside, their humble dream has been for centuries and is still is now, the dream of a full rice-bowl and a roof over their heads. The many who had been turfed out of their homes and properties to make way for modernization, have the same dream: a fair compensation for the confiscation of their properties, a full rice-bowl and a roof over their heads.

Out of a population of 1.4 billion, 45% live in the cities. The modern China we are familiar with is mainly that of the urbanized Chinese and, naturally, those connected with the government. The affluence they enjoy can be traced back to official corruption and a zealous adherence to Deng Xiaoping's song of joy—"To make money is glorious!" It used to be a case of "when America sneezes, the rest of the world catches a cold." No more so. Today, we are anxious because when China sneezes, the rest of the world may catch the deadly flu.

The impressive extravaganza of the Beijing Olympics Opening Ceremony dwelt, quite significantly, on the extravaganza of China's traditional past glory. For modern China, the digital and technological age is the age of enlightenment and progress. The man-in-the street gets a glimpse of the sumptuous feast available outside China and they know that they too, have the right to partake of this wonder. Democracy is the conduit for challenging the government of the day, freedom of speech is on their side; human rights are their birth right and they want them NOW!

I know that father would applaud with delightful pride. He might, however, have grave concerns regarding the issue of morality and responsibility. The lucky youth in China today are not dissimilar to the youth in developed countries with their self-centred "Me only" mentality overriding everything else that could raise some Chinese eyebrows. Oh dear! Where is the great Sage whose teaching has galvanized the Chinese world for four thousand years? Throughout the ages, generations of Chinese have sifted and accepted the best and most practical of his teachings in order to survive. Will this practice continue? To father, a reformed modernized China must have a place for Confucius. This could possibly be a controversial issue. I suppose, in father's eyes, a Chinese is a Confucianist is a Chinese. Confucius' teaching has been pivotal to moulding that Chinese mind which has the largesse to absorb different religions, teachings and philosophies as long as they contribute to the common good and the noble. Honour, Responsibility and Respect should be the badge of pride of a Confucianist Chinese.

Those on the seat of the previous government led by Hu Jintao, facing the challenge of modernization with a whole set of new ideologies. are my contemporaries whose immediate predecessors had bourn the pain of China's humiliation. These are the people whose parents' traditional Chinese education has moulded their thought and outlook, the effect of which still lingers on. In today's China, however, people under the age of forty-five perhaps, may regard the concept of ethics, such as courtesy and respect for elders and authority as rather quaint and outmoded. Will the money-conscious China of today have a place for Confucius? It is interesting to note that in traditional China, the merchant class was in the lowest strata of the Confucian social hierarchy. Today, a rich Chinese is invariably involved in business and trading. The current government can feel very happy with this, but may not be so ready to deal with the vexed question of human rights and the right to rebel.

On the question of today's sexual revolution, the face of the father in my dream seemed to have gone a weird shade of purple. Thank goodness that the matter of civil disobedience brought back the smiles as he quoted from Mencius, (one of Confucius' brightest students):

"Reverent disobedience is permissible when the command is wrong, a son should resist his father and a minister should resist his August Master." Mencius went so far as to believe that it is one's sacred duty to rebel against a bad ruler. What enchanting music to the Democracy crowd!

Through the looking glass of the dying breed, the current older generation, the intergenerational conflict in China perhaps appears to pose a demanding challenge. Today's youth are spared the baggage of the past—the Opium Wars and the Middle Kingdom concept are too alien, too "far out" to comprehend. The wired world that they revel in today is the NOW world. It is "cool" to be at one with their counterparts in the developed countries outside their own. They are proud to be computer nerds; they too, want to swirl in the delirium of "heavy metal", Punk Rock music and life style. If the "mental-as-anything" gyrations and screaming of a tortured soul of their art and music seem to the older generation to reflect the miasma of an undisciplined world, then it has become their problem. They have to adapt and have patience . . . .

"Yes," father nodded smilingly. "Make haste slowly"—I think that was what he was muttering before he vanished.

The Chinese government has reason to move with the times. This was highlighted in the spectacular Opening Ceremony of the 2008 Beijing Olympics. The country that believes in selective blockage and censorship of the internet has reason to be grateful for this smart invention. As much as the internet has become an invisible weapon of the younger breed who have a different set of values and enjoy a less glamorous lifestyle comparable to that of their Western counterpart, this very self-same internet with its Facebook, its blogs, its twitters etc., has been the very conduit that has succeeded in boosting the popularity of the government. It has shielded them from some situations that might have been very threatening had the Confucian ideology of loss of "Mandate to Rule" been accepted as a matter of course. In the past, Emperors had to answer for any natural disasters which hit the country; they were construed as evidence that Heaven was showing their subjects that the Emperors had lost their "Mandate to Rule"

In 2008, several natural disasters hit China, the most serious of which was the Sichuan earthquake which displaced several million people and caused over 7000 deaths. Official corruption resulting in shonky buildings had been a factor contributing to the heavy toll. Yet the government did not lose its mandate to rule. Thanks to the smart media propaganda and the internet, President Hu Jintao, Uncle Hu to his admiring subjects, was portrayed as a caring and very human uncle to his grieving nation.

China's prosperity and strength today could well be traced to the abject humiliation of the Celestial Empire as a result of the Opium Wars. Any and every country tried to have a piece of the once insulated empire—even little Japan was able to grab her share of the pie. People of my parents' generation still carried this baggage of shame throughout their lives. China had to stand up again and hold her head high.

*9 The Carving of China.

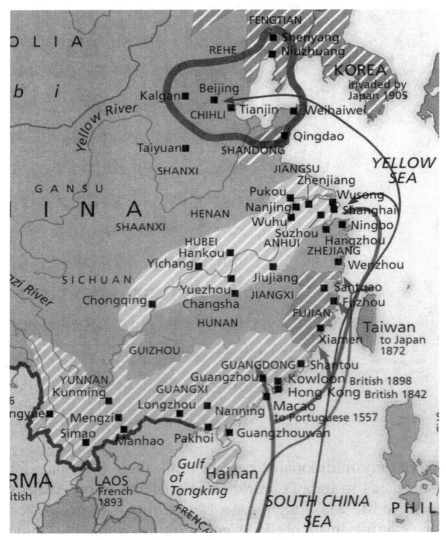

*10 Close-up of ports affected by the Opium Wars.

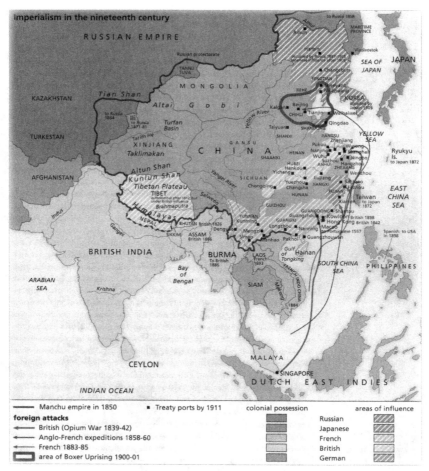

*[11] China after the Opium Wars.

Would my traditionalist parents think there is a place for Confucius in today's world? The students in my father's teenage life who fought for a New China had recognized that Confucianism needed some scrutiny. Would the China of today, which seems to be somewhat disillusioned with the past, take another look at Confucianism in an attempt to provide some anchorage in this heady tide of mercurial changes and the ruthless pursuit of the almighty dollar?

Will there be a need for some signposts pointing in the direction of Confucian values such as Love, Respect, Responsibility and a sense of Discipline? Scholar Kang Xiaoguang the country's top advocate for Confucian education seems to think so. He complained that the society in today's China is at its worst ever. The need for some moral standard seems so clear. I can see that familiar twinkle in father's eyes because he knows that in 2008, about six million copies of the Confucian Analects were sold in China. Patience! Yes, we need patience!

Father knows that Mr Hu Jintao may be looking for inspiration from the Sage as well. Confucian education is already in the school syllabus and major universities are offering courses in Confucian Philosophy. Mr Hu's government may also benefit in adopting the benign face of the Old Sage to counteract the image of a rapacious juggernaut. It is obvious that the challenge of utilizing the teaching of the Sage to stabilize the social climate of the day would be gargantuan. Confucius teaching pivots on establishing world harmony. It emphasizes the subjugation of self for the common good; one has to place one's individual interest last. This is surely gibberish to the XYZ generations and we may have to draw a deep breath when we ponder on the Alpha generation. It may be as real as asking the corrupt officials to hand over their ill-gotten earnings to charity. However, the important first step . . . .

Humankind is resilient and adaptable to change. My traditionalist parents changed, their contemporaries did as well; so did our predecessors. Father's smile heralds the positive to come. The Sage had said: " . . . If a gentleman departs from humanity, how can he bear the name? Not even for the lapse of a single meal does a gentleman ignore humanity. In moments of haste, he cleaves to it; in seasons of peril he cleaves to it."*12

Confucius' "humanity" and altruism can be with us even when we are rushing in the fast lane of today. This is most evident in times of tragedies.

The Chinese pigtails of father's day are non-existent in today's China, an outcome of a China which had fought for the teaching of Science and Mathematics in order to have a fighting chance against the colonial powers. It is interesting to note that many Chinese students nowadays, seem to veer towards a Commerce / Accountancy and Business degree. Their prowess in mathematics is evidently far beyond this:

A go-between offered her match-making service to a young couple's baby girl. This aroused the baby's father to anger.

He expostulated: "Oh no! My daughter is one year old and this boy is two. By the time my daughter is ten, this boy will be twenty years old. I don't want my son-in-law to be twice my daughter's age!"

His helpful wife intervened: "You are wrong husband! Our daughter is one year old this year. Next year she will be two years old—a perfect match for the boy! Please don't reject this service."

CHAPTER 8

"O MY LUVE'S LIKE A RED, RED ROSE."

It was a pristine blue-sky day when we showed off the beauty of the Gold Coast to our visitor from overseas. We had been looking forward to a picnic lunch and a quiet drink on this perfect day complete with surfs and healthy surfers when who should turn up, but a little bald-headed man setting up a little table and a loud speaker right in front of us, which obstructed our splendid view. My dismay must have been palpable to the maximum degree, for in no time, the sprightly little man complete with coat and tie raced to inform us that he was a marriage celebrant, ready to conduct a marriage. Right on cue, with the blue sky and green sea backdrop, a cluster of well-dressed guests happily gathered to greet the bride, all dressed in white, accompanied by four beautiful bridesmaids.

A fellow spectator made a comment to me that it was just so good to hear a marriage vow again.

"There seem to be so few and far between these days," she said; "people just prefer to shack up, don't they?"

I wasted no time in providing the moral support in registering my unease about the term "partners" for couples who seem reluctant to accept a firm commitment of being a registered spouse. I have often wondered if this was a strategy to have a convenient exit route because people nowadays fight shy of this business of "in health and in sickness . . . . and unto death do us part" promise. I imagine the thought of having to go through a divorce could be a strong deterrent. It can be an expensive and messy procedure. The only party who seems to profit by it is the lawyer who is ever ready to welcome his client. There was an enterprising legal firm in Britain which provided very helpful and encouraging assistance to couples whose marriage hit turbulent waters. This firm offered a £220/ voucher and a "must-have" present in 2009 with another enticing bonus of a free half to one hour free advice with a lawyer. It is quite touching to know that some species in the bird kingdom are brave enough to face the travail of a divorce to remain loyally bound to each other for life when they start a family. The albatross, for one, enjoys a life-span of about fifty years and remains faithfully married to each other till "unto death do us part." How refreshing it is to see husband and wife taking turns to look after the young ones!

Far more disturbing is this trend of a "one-night stand". It is a chilling fact that this trendy habit seems to be so contagious as to have a hold on the urban "modern, progressive" youth in developing countries round the world. The four Fs—"Find them, fondle them, f . . k them" and "forget" them seem to be a badge of esteem and the more nonchalantly it is tossed off during a conversation, the more "cool" one is regarded.

The darkening cloud on father's face loomed ominously from the void . . . . Yes, I do, I do remember father's opinion on the matter of love and life-long commitment to one's spouse. I still remember the story of the use of the garden well in a traditional Chinese home. The little girl in my childhood days had been fearfully riveted to stories of horrible honour killing . . . father had recounted tales about the value of women chastity in the traditional Chinese world and the type of punishment an unchaste daughter could face—she would be thrown and buried in the family well by the parents. The cloud that shadowed father's face at that time was one of shock and sorrow when he told us the romanticized story of one Li K'uei whom father admired.

Li K'uei, was a big man, physically head and shoulder above other men. His bravery was legendary; he was an honest and good worker being able to carry loads that needed three men's effort. It was a snowy day when the earth and the sky were merged into an indistinguishable white curtain. The landlord's only daughter with coiffured hair and jade hair pins, bent over her embroidery was conscious of shadowy movements of men at work in the yard outside. Suddenly her attention was caught by a shadowy apparition emerging from a billowing puff of steam. This configured into a big man seemingly draped with strips of seaweed over his semi-naked body. Li K'uei, bent double with a heavy load of timber was striding in ankle-deep snow. Shocked by the sight of this, she immediately summoned one of her maids to bring her her father's discarded coat which she threw out of the window to the semi-naked man. Unfortunately when her father noticed Li K'uei in his old coat and learnt where it had come from, he thundered into the house for an explanation from his daughter. His fury blinded him to all the protestations of innocence from his daughter, wife and the kneeling maids. The demon in his eyes pointed to one fact and one fact alone—his daughter had brought eternal shame to his family and she had to face the just dessert— to be thrown into the family well which was to be filled in to bury the stigma. The expression on father's face made a memorable impression on the little girl; it was one etched with sorrow and disgust. Father did value chastity in women, but he did not condone barbaric punishment.

Father's romantic ideal was that of a love match. He too, sighed for the magic old time of "eternal love" so well immortalized by Robert Burns (1759-1796) in:

> O my luve's like a red, red rose
>   That's newly sprung in June:
> O my luve's like the melodie
>   That's sweetly played in tune.
>
> As fair art thou, my bonnie lass,
>   So deep in luve am I:
> And I will luve thee till, my dear,
>   Till a' the seas gang dry . . .

Unfortunately there are still some people who don't have the privilege of "falling in love" The culture of match-making is still very much alive today; in remote areas of Asian countries which seem to be caught in a time-warp. The positive way of looking at this seeming barbaric practice is, I suppose, that in the absence of a "boy-meets-girl" treat, the lucky satisfied arranged marriage couples would count their blessing and strive to make the marriage a permanent commitment. The fact that a divorce was a social stigma was certainly a helpful incentive for one to accept an unhappy marriage. This attitude was based on the Chinese belief that "marriages are made in heaven." The unhappy wife would have to make the best of a bad situation while the dissatisfied husband would cheerfully choose the outlet of keeping concubines—as many as he could afford them.

An arranged marriage, especially when it was match-made in traditional China would generally mean that both the bride and groom could only be seeing each other for the first time on their wedding day. The groom's anxiety in this case would be a more prolonged one—his chance of seeing the bride would only come on the wedding night in the bridal chamber when he lifted the heavy head-gear and veil of his bride. This heavy ornamental headgear was more than an endurance test for the bride—it was to do with propriety and modesty. It was deemed improper for a bride to cast her eyes about in the presence of male company on her wedding day. Hopefully, keeping the head bowed could give the bride some physical relief from the strain of the weight. Father used to narrate tales of young brides in danger of suffocating to death in the airless, heavily curtained sedan chairs in hot summers when the abject beings were slowly rocked to insanity in a long, hot arduous journey to face their bridegrooms. There had been tales of brides finding their grooms to be imbeciles or physically deformed after a torturous journey. Thanks to the unscrupulous match-makers who knew how to exploit the system! A resilient victim of this tragic situation would accept this as his or her karma.

Buddhism has a panacea for this type of situation—it would be taken as "just pure bad luck"—one has to accept this "fate". Self-flagellation would begin with a self-imposed consolation that the unfortunate current situation is a penalty for one's "sins" of the past life and that things would improve in the next reincarnation.

Since a marriage in the Chinese world has, ideally, to be binding for life, some parents would go to great lengths to resort to checking with fortune-tellers or turn to astrology for enlightenment on the couple's compatibility. A detailed study of the couples' dates of birth would offer some suggestion as to the auspicious day and time for marriage to counteract any form of incompatibility or bad luck. One such reference is the Chinese animal horoscopes which calculation is based on the Moon—or rather, on lunar years. The Chinese lunar year comprises twelve New Moons, with a thirteenth added on every dozen years. This explains why Chinese New Year Day never falls on the same date. As with Western signs of the Zodiacs, the cycle is also a series of twelve—twelve years instead of twelve months. Each year of the Chinese horoscopes is represented by an animal and this animal would exercise an influence on the lives, destiny and character of the person born in that year.

The popular story was that one New Year's Day, the Lord Buddha summoned the animals in the world to appear before him. Only twelve animals turned up and these were rewarded with having a year named after them—in the order of their arrival. The first to arrive was the rat; piggy came last. Since it is a twelve-year cycle, one could easily calculate a person's age when one knows the animal year she was born.

The cycle is as follows:

The rat	1900,1912
The buffalo	1901;1913
The tiger	1902;1914
The rabbit	1903;1915
The dragon	1904;1916
The snake	1905;1917
The horse	1906;1918
The goat	1907;1919
The monkey	1908;1920
The rooster	1909;1921
The dog	1910;1922
The pig	1911;1923.

The animal influence on one's life is naturally of symbolic significance; the rooster, for example, would have to use his claws to scratch for food—the person born under this sign would be expected to have to work for his living. The pig is a good liver, often a sensualist. He is naive, of a good nature but hides plenty of will power and authority. He trusts no-one; and wisely so! On the matter of compatibility, it would be obvious that one born in the year of the rat would be wise to give a wide berth of the person born in the year of the snake. This should be taken as a simplistic and very general gauge; one's characteristic is, however, further determined by the season, the month, the day, right down to the very minute of birth.

I have often wondered how a morally-responsible man like my father, (indeed, how his contemporaries) would handle today's scenario of elastic relationship. It would be a totally alien planet for them if they were to find themselves in one of our nocturnal "cages" on a weekend where many of the single men and women, jostling cheek by jowl, ostensibly to enjoy an evening of drinks have one common mission—a hunt for a sexual mate. It would be interesting to witness my parents' reaction to our current attitude to sex and the acceptance of a "one-night-stand".

Though traditional China had a rigid attitude towards women chastity, it had never been the practice of throwing a man into a well for besmirching the family reputation either from the loss of his virginity or his being unfaithful to his wife. It seemed to be a universal right for a young man "to sow his wild oats" and of course, in some countries, it has always been acceptable for a man to have more than one wife. In traditional China, the number of wives and concubines a man had was a proud advertisement of his virility and wealth. Traditional Chinese society expected a woman to remain faithful to her spouse unto death. To remain a widow, irrespective of her age was something to be lauded. There had even been instances of young betrothed women entering the nunnery on the death of their fiancé. The reward for such sacrifices was celebrated in "The Biographies of Heroic Women"—a collection of accounts of exemplary women in antiquity written by an eminent scholar, Liu Xiang (79-8 BC). Chastity for a woman was a heavy price to pay—what price for tribute such as this—"Song of a Chaste Wife" by Chang Chi (c768-830) of the Tang Dynasty.

A married woman was given a pair of pearls by her admirer. She lovingly treasured them for one night—

"I wore them over my red gauze bodice"

before she returned them to the admirer reminding him that her duty as a wife was to remain faithful to her husband till death.

"I know, sir, that your heart is pure as the sun and the moon . . .
I now return your two shining pearls with a tear on each,
Regretting that we did not meet while I was still unwed."[*1]

One of the encouragements given to my mother to marry a much older man was the consolation that she would be spared the ordeal of having to dance attendance on a mother-in-law—the mother-in-law was too far away in China and mum would be safe in Malaysia! The reputation of mothers-in-law in traditional China had often been notorious. One of the pictures I came across was that of a hatchet face of a mother-in-law sitting erect on a ponderous tortoise shell-carved cedar wood chair with her maid servants in attendance. She was sitting outside the bridal bedroom. She had the important duty of letting the young marrieds in the bedroom know that they must "hurry up and get on with it!" because she expected one of the maids to come out of the bridal chamber with a stained white bed sheet. Woe betides the poor girl if the sheet had not been discoloured. Judging by the sheer expression of this particular mother-in-law, I presume the young couples could count themselves "lucky" that the formidable dragon-lady did not demand keeping her sacred vigil IN the bedroom. It appeared that some versatile young people could cheat by staining the bed sheet with animal gore. At such times, they would need to have the full loyalty of the maids.

Father had narrated many stories of wicked mothers-in-law. Following Confucius' code of conduct, the in-laws always lived with their first-born sons for life. The poor daughter-in-law would be kept in life-long servitude to her husband's family, and God help her if the family was a big one with sisters-in-law to contend with. Needless to say, the daughter-in-law's first priority was to serve her parents-in-law before serving her husband and master. The mother-in-law needed special attention of course. With the absence of running tap water, the married slave's first duty was to bring a basin of warm water for the august lady's morning ablution. While the dowager and family had breakfast, the dutiful slave would be seen to clean the in-law's bedroom starting with the chamber pot. Boredom would never be a worry—the house-keeping chores would shield her from that. She could count her blessings if the mother-in-law retired early to bed to release her to the privacy of her own bedchamber.

Uncharitable presentation of wicked mothers-in-law seemed to stem from the inherent system of stringent expectation of duties of wives of their sons. Unfortunately, cases were rife of many of these down-trodden wives living for the day when they, in their turn, could lord over their own daughters-in-law. Traditional attitude to women had been far from flattering; much had been expected of the weaker sex. The earliest Chinese poetry on women originated from the early Zhou period (1100-722BC). At important court ceremonies, poems from the Book of Songs (Shijing) would be selected to be sung. One of these odes highlights the distrust of women—especially those involved in politics and affairs of state—

> Clever men build cities,
> Clever women topple them.
> Beautiful these clever women may be
> But they are owls and kites.
> Women have long tongues
> That lead to ruin.
> Disorder does not come down from heaven;
> It is produced by women.[*2]

However, there are historical records of events and tales celebrating the supreme sacrifices and courage of women. Father was strong in his tribute to such persons. One such famous character was Hua Mulan who ventured going to war on behalf of her aged father, dressed up as a man. Her exploits and military skill won her great recognition and she was posthumously honoured with the Xiao Lie General award in the Tang Dynasty.

There is some historical confusion and claims relating to her surname; albeit, Hua Mulan has become a household traditional Chinese heroine. The popular accepted view was that she came from the region known as the Central Plains, of Hu Liang Prefecture, in Gansu. The story of her life has been celebrated in poems and operas. I remember one such opera in the film version that father took us to had a packed audience which clearly revelled in a Hollywood-tainted splendour of the traditional opera. The popular version of the story was that Mulan's father, an aging fearsome General had always bemoaned the fact that he did not have a son old enough to fight for his country in his stead. His other son was too young and Mulan was only a female. Then the dreaded day dawned—the old father was summoned to battle by the Emperor. Mulan's previous pleas to her father to let her go in his place had fallen on deaf ears—it was too preposterous a request for contemplation

Traditional military service was exclusively a male domain; military life was Spartan, if not cruel. Boys had to be trained by experts from a young age. The art of warfare relied heavily on hand-to-hand combat, an expert handling of an array of various instruments of war, and a mastery of horsemanship. Steel helmets, heavy breast plates and coats of mail, not dissimilar to the counterparts of the contemporary Western World, were the mandatory uniforms. Popular operas and films employ a spectacular combination of gymnastic and acrobatic skills popularized by the "invincible" kung fu maestro, Bruce Lee of the 1960s' era. Hollywood ostentatious display aside, Chinese traditional combat did rely heavily on acrobatic agility.

How Mulan gained the permission of her parents to enter this bloody theatre of war was idealized in the extravaganza of a competition duel between a young man and the expert swordsman, Mulan's father. The scene of the duel itself was worth queuing up for the performance:

> The heavy blades clashed,
> The bright sparks flew,
> The swordsmen panted and grunted.
> The heroes plunged,
> The heroes lunged,
> All dusty and blood-encrusted.
> In the dying echoes of the crashing din
> And swirling dust a-thinning,
> One and only one victor was a-standing . . . .
> The young challenger.

When the majestic warrior collapsed to his knees, he had the humility to congratulate the young swordsman and paid him the supreme compliment that he would gladly die if he had a son like him—. The young man discarded his coat of mail:

> And there before him in youthful glow,
> Stood his one beautiful daughter—
> The daughter whose birth was a wasteful bother.

Mulan knelt to ask for his pardon.

Known as The Lady General in Chinese History, Mulan led her men to victory after victory. How she managed to disguise her sex in those years of battle could easily be a matter for a doctorate research. The fact that Mulan had kept secret the very arduous combat training to arrive at where she was, an invincible General, was indeed a feat of gargantuan stature. That she had to go into battle encumbered with the heavy coat of mail and steel helmet in command of a fearsome all-male army was a miracle indeed.

I imagine that the heavy military armour itself would preclude any female participation. The little girl who listened to such stories of valour with open-mouthed awe was very grateful to be born a girl. Yes, a useless girl, she had come to a definite conclusion that she would be too happy to empty chamber pots in addition to scrubbing all pots and pans in servile gratitude if just to be spared falling over herself while clanging about in the heavy armour. To be butchered in a bloody battle was one nightmare, to have to face the Emperor's edict—"Off with his head!" in failing to answer the call to battle would certainly traumatize her very physical growth had she been fated to be a son in those days of yore. Yep! That little girl sighed in cozy gratitude that *her* severed head would not have to grace the city gate for not dancing to the war tune of her emperor!

Mulan's gift to her father was a supreme sacrifice of filial piety. She had superseded any son's effort to immortalize his family name.

My constant reference to father's reaction to what is happening in today's world is an attempt at looking at how CHANGE affects all generations, in all matters and at all times. Today's rapid evolution of electronic marvels and social transformation seem to swirl at a giddy speed. Computerized and electronic gadgets of "yesterday" can very quickly become junk today—newer, faster, smarter gadgets edge their way in. We have come a long way even in the space of one decade—our ipods, mobile phones, to name just the most common "must haves" are all smarter and "faster" and bring about a miraculous transformation to our lives, more astounding and far more dramatic in shaping our life style. The Great Industrial Revolution of the last age seems to pale into insignificance. The heritage and romanticized splendor of father's traditional China is fast fading into obscurity. The China of today is focused on economic supremacy; the youth of today are too mesmerized by the magic of a fast-moving digital transformation to be bothered with past heritage which is considered archaic and possibly meaningless.

We have changed—change is always inevitable—the Lord Buddha propounds that life is an illusion. Father and his contemporaries might think that today's world is an illusion too, they would marvel at how the sexes' roles are so naturally interchangeable today—a topsy-turvy version of the Confucian world that they were familiar with. We have house-husbands and families bidding farewell to wives and mothers marching off to face the bullets and bombs in a war zone. Our present-day Mulans do not have to resort to subterfuge to prove their ability to serve in battle. "The place of woman is in the home" appears to be fast becoming an anachronism. Now that it seems necessary to have a two-income family, we are lucky to live in the time when jobs are not gender-based and naturally we are proud of the women who have touched the glass ceiling in an all-male domain. Is it Buddha's axiom on the "happy medium" which produces that enigmatic smile of serenity? He knows that women can go that far and that far only; there is a line in the sand somewhere which should be observed to get the best governance in society. There are certain things that men are better at and vice versa. A mother's role is unique and will always be invaluable. Looming from that void was that satisfied chuckle from father with that sonorous mutter that a woman's valued role as a wife and mother must not be underestimated.

My mother was given away in marriage at age twenty-one to our father of whom she knew nothing about. The arranged marriage had been a solid, sound relationship. Father naturally slid into the Confucian male role of "hunter", provider and protector of his family. Mother, lacking the privilege of an education and professional qualification was magnificent in her natural role of mother and wife. No remonstrance, no competition—it is therefore not difficult to see why Chinese men, in fact, Asian men in general, have qualms about marrying an "intelligent" educated woman. Emasculation of the male should be avoided at all costs—so they like to believe. In the case of our family, our father seemed to be the odd man out; he was the one who had to "assimilate". A man fresh from China with Classical learning and traditional values, father and the rest of his family had some difficulties understanding each other. To father's dismay, our Chinese dialect naturally includes some bastardization of Malay words, which invited father's jocular derision that we were uncultured apes. Albeit, our mother's wisdom and common sense approach to life had won father's respect and appreciation. Father always found it necessary to resort to consulting with her on matters of import.

It used to amuse me to see father in the role of a humble, submissive husband when he would wring his hands while chuckling in apologetic good humour stuttering: "Old wife . . ." (An irritating habit of Chinese husbands of that era to address even their newly married brides as "old wife"). "Old wife, heh! heh!" chuckled father self-consciously as he hovered about the kitchen, "You will produce a miracle as always, yes? Old wife, you are a miracle yourself . . ." That his agitated visit to the kitchen for the hundredth time to peer over mother's cooking did not drive mother to insanity was a miracle in itself.

This happened to be an oft-repeated performance whenever father decided to invite his friends to dinner. We were not as well-off as some of father's friends then, and father would inevitably end up with too little food supply to warrant the lavishness he hoped to provide for the number of guests. Poor father's only hope seemed to be on his efficacious wife who somehow or other, managed at all times to save his face. Mother's culinary skill became quite legendary. The dinners, often lively with father's efflorescent good humour were often appreciated with warm compliments to the self-effacing cook. Father's glow of pride in his wife was something worth struggling for. It was at times like this that mother lived up to her name which literal meaning was "should be precious." Mother was truly precious indeed.

Father was proud of his love of the Classics. We did find father's educated accent quite quaint. I loved listening to the beautiful cadences especially when he recited classical poems, his head swaying and nodding in rhythm to the text. His children were naturally encouraged to attend

Chinese schools; to keep the Chinese culture alive, so to say. Only a couple of my siblings had the opportunity to attain an O level of Chinese education which was not of significant values anyway—no in-depth education on the Classics and Culture. The Chinese School-leaving Certificate offered no guarantee of a job in British Malaya then; only an English education had this opportunity. People with a Chinese education would normally end up in the line of business and trade, compliments of the Chinese net-work and Benevolent Associations. This scenario has not changed in today's Malaysia; a Chinese School-leaving Certificate is fit for the bin; a Malay qualification for a Chinese offers no guarantee of a job either, the intake into the Malay Government and public service is mainly reserved for the ethnic Malays—the bumiputras, "sons of the soil."

Our early Chinese teacher was father, who, in instilling into us a sense of duty and responsibility as expected of a moral human being, utilised the art of enticement to get us to the magic casement that opened unto us the glory of a golden past. He naturally embellished his teaching with palatable servings of myths and legends of valour and love, which he often dramatised to our delight. He read us beautiful poems which cadences captivated my imagination and I loved listening to them though their full meaning and significance eluded me. Inspiring tales of valour glorified our past heroes, but to me, it was the tales of the supreme sacrifices and pathos of women, shimmering in the gossamer of the visionary past that lent them an air of enduring enchantment. Songs of eternal sorrow laced the lives of women of all strata in life. Chinese Literature is rich with stories which glorify the roles of courtesans. One of the most poignant of such tales written in the imitation of the art of the colloquial story-teller was the known as "The Courtesan's Jewel Box".

The story centred round a wasteful young scholar. Li Chia, son of a provincial official and Tu Shi-niang, a beautiful, gifted girl who was a courtesan. Though Tu Shi-niang was courted by many young men of rich and noble families, she became attached to Li Chia; the more so when he had squandered all his money in "the house of flowers and willows;" (euphemism for brothel). The handsome, amiable youth was in a sorry state indeed—he had no courage to face the father who had allocated him the fund for the pursuit of scholarship. Tired of the vacuous glitz and glamour of her life, all Tu Shi-niang dreamt for was a quiet, happy marriage to the man she loved—Li Chia. With assiduous saving and some cash borrowed from a friend, she managed to ransom herself from the house of flowers and willows to pursue her dream.

Their plan was to hire a boat to seek a temporary dwelling before summoning enough courage to face the father. While waiting to cross the Yangtze, Li Chia struck up an acquaintance with a young salt merchant, Sun Fu, whose boat was moored next to theirs. Sun Fu captivated by the beauty of the young wife made an offer of 1000 ounces of silver for her. He volunteered the seductive advice to the scholar that he could use the silver to placate his father. When Li Chia informed his wife of his acceptance of the deal that night, Tu Shih-niang accepted her fate in dignified silence.

Early next morning, she bedecked herself in her best finery and appeared on deck. In the presence of her husband and Sun Fu, in view of the bustling crowd by the river, Tu Shi-niang opened the jewel box she was carrying. To the astonishment of everyone, she spilled into the river all the drawers of glittering jewels, gold and jade ornaments, pearls and emeralds of all shades and colours, the likes of which took one's breath away. The shocked gasp from the crowd was like a mighty gush of wind through the woods.

Li Chia, overcame with shame and remorse rushed to clasp his wife to his heart. Tu Shi-niang pushed him aside and confronting Sun Fu, she berated him for shattering her dream:

"How dare you still covet 'the joys of the pillow and mat'—(euphemism for love-making)—with me?" to the hiss and curses of the crowd.

She then turned to Li Chia and said:

"During these many years of 'dust and breeze'—(euphemism for prostitution)—I have privately amassed enough savings to support myself for the rest of my life. Ever since I met you, we have sworn by mountain and sea an oath of fidelity unto our old age." She reminded him that her savings in the depth of the river was about 10,000 ounces of silver more than sufficient to placate his father and to enable them to enjoy a splendid future in love and marriage. In painful bitterness, she told him that she could not believe that his fidelity was so shallow as to induce him to desert her for a paltry sum of silver in that early stage of their journey.

"There is jade in my chest but I regret you have no pearls in your eyes. Ill-starred is my luck that just after I have escaped from the toils and woes of 'the dust and breeze', I should have met with desertion at your hands!"

The crowd moved to tears swore and spat at the two men. Li Chia, on his knees, tearfully grasped at Tu-Shiniang's gown while begging her for forgiveness. She swerved aside and grasping the jewel box, she leapt into the dark depth of the river. Yells for help from the crowd and effort to retrieve Shiniang failed. She had vanished without a trace below the billowing swells.

"Pitiful indeed was this famed courtesan, as pretty as flower or jade, to be thus suddenly buried in the bellies of the river fish.

> Her three souls returned dimly to the watery main;
> And her seven spirits entered forlorn the road to the
> Shades.""*3

CHAPTER 9

THE DISHONOURABLE "THOUSAND GOLD"

Being a dinosaur as far as alien things are concerned, I find myself adrift in Wonderland. This digital world with its ever-lengthening list of marvels such as cyber space, MySpace, Facebook Youtube, blogs, ipads, ipods and on and on has become an impossible labyrinth for me to negotiate. Suffice it for me to give a blanket confession that my heart goes out to the many grandparents and parents of today who have to cope with the "alien world" of the younger generation. This sub-culture group has even its own lingo which is more impregnable than any fortress!

Some years back, I came upon a clip about a youth boasting to a Senior about this Smart Age of TV., jet planes, space travel, nuclear energy, cell phones, computer and all the high-tech gadgets which allow information to travel at the speed of light. He then sneeringly asked the Senior: "And what have you done?"

"We invented them!" he retorted. I could hear my father's voice here.

Change and progress in time inevitably pushes each receding older generation to the back seat, but they have the wisdom to "go with the flow". Our parents in their alien world of Malaya in the last century also got quite lost. They decided to give us the choice to be English or Chinese-educated. Father's encouragement, however, was for us to be English-educated just to ensure a better future for us. They were fully aware of the gamble they were taking—a generation gap with a language difference resulting in a clash of cultures could produce a fearsome schism between parent and child. Since the need to retain one's heritage is an important matter, my parents had every intention of giving their children an opportunity to receive private tuition in Chinese.

This need was especially so back then when they were still in their traditional straitjacket. The China they had left behind had a strong negative racist attitude towards all Europeans. The English, for historical reasons had been awarded the top grade for racial slur.

The term "FOLANGI" was the neutral term used by the Chinese for Europeans. It derived from the Arab word "FERINGHI" coined to designate the FRANKS in the time of the Crusades. In the 16th Century rumours ran rife in Southern China that there was a hairy species of smelly people whom they referred to as "the Foreign Devils" or "Barbarians". These aggressive specimens were noted to be arrogant, ferocious, uncouth and bloodthirsty, reaching for their swords on the slightest pretext. They were alleged to have come from across the many oceans in the direction of the setting sun to disturb the tranquil conduct of trade.

In my parents' day, the stigma attached to these terms was still quite real. Father's contempt for this hairy species was quite eloquent when he would admonish us at meal times: "Don't use your fingers! You have the chopsticks! We are not barbarians, we have etiquette . . ." Father disliked the "foreign devils" for their "lack of elegance and sophistication," because they use knives and forks at meals.

The terms "Western Barbarians" and "Red Haired Devils" had a specific poisonous connotation in the era of the Opium Wars, which began in 1840. By now, they certainly have lost their sting; in fact, they have become neutral words. I am always amused when my contemporaries and the younger generation in the family who have lived in Brisbane and graduated from the Queensland University still use these terms as a matter of course. No tinge of rancour or spite at all—they are just a convenient terms.

Meanwhile, our parents knew that they had to assimilate to survive. Just like the bamboo that gracefully complements the solidity and strength of a rock, as depicted in popular Chinese brush painting, our parents' practice in this case had always been that there are times when one should be like the bamboo—beautiful, graceful, steadfast and strong because of its flexibility to bend with the wind and yet to remain upright in dignity. They bent with the wind.

Father, who had a solid traditional Chinese education was very much aware that our sense of who we are and from whence we come, would never be complete unless we understand and, indeed, respect the spirit of past ages and appreciate our heritage. Language holds the key to this; it is the life-blood of one's culture. However, mindful of the evolution of change, our parents showed us the need to adopt an intelligent and selective adherence to what is for the common good. That did not stop father from reminding us that "we are Chinese!" whenever we misbehaved. (What came to my mind was something as amusing as the saying, "No sex, please. We are British!) It was certainly no laughing matter to father, however. This was a weighty admonishment meaning that our behaviour was abominable, shameful and ignoble. "As if being Chinese is so lofty!" we scoffed, silently of course.

We had often been reminded that culture and tradition define our ethnicity and our uniqueness which could be temptingly submerged into oblivion in our alien environment. "Don't you forget that!" he shook his authoritative finger at us. The British Philosopher Bhikhu Parekh argues: "Since human beings are culturally embedded, respect for them entails respect for their cultures and ways of life." My parents were wise enough to accept that it is normal instinct for Man to live within his culture, but that there should be room for flexibility and assimilation, especially when one has to cope with an alien environment.

There seemed to be two categories of Chinese immigrants in Malaya in those days. There was the traditional Chinese-educated Chinese such as my father who had only recently extricated himself from a China still in the throes of its agonizing rebirth as a New China. Then there was the other category of earlier Chinese immigrants, to which my mother belonged. My mother had left China at the tender age of nine to be brought up by her relatives in Malaya, a non-Chinese-educated family. This group was known as "Babas" or "Nyonyas". Generally, this category of Chinese was regarded as un-Chinese in respect of their lack of a traditional Chinese education. Their assimilation into the Malay society was reflected in their attire—Malay sarongs and loose tunics and pseudo-Chinese cuisine. Snooty papa did not hold these people in high regard—"barbarians!" "half-baked Chinese!" he would mutter between gritted teeth. This latter term was an honour he conferred on my good-natured mother when he was in that mood of fatherly benevolence and sweet tolerance. I am sure that when father had to deal with his children, he must have secretly thanked his lot that this "half-baked" wife of his, with her gentle ways, was a boon by comparison. His children, alas! found his dialect quaint and too scholarly to comprehend and they thought being a "barbarian" was good fun!

The Ying and Yang energies complemented each other superbly in my parents' relationship. When father was intractable, mother was sweet reason itself. Father's dynamism, impulsiveness and bubbling sense of mischievous humour reminded me of the Fire element in contrast to my mother's quiet sobriety and amicability. Mother often chose to remain as placid as a pool, quietly but sprightly sparkling in the reflection of the moon. It was interesting that her very serenity would often bring about a sweet, meek concession from my father in times of conflict. The very self-effacing characteristic of her stoicism reminded me of the power of the water element.

"Nothing is weaker than water,
But when it attacks something hard
Or resistant, then nothing withstands it,
   And nothing will alter its way.

Everyone knows this, that weakness prevails
Over strength and that gentleness conquers
   The adamant hindrance of men . . ."[*1]

Mother with her ready laughter had other surprises for me—After father's death, at about age sixty, she decided to come to live with me when I migrated to Australia in the seventies. This was her first time in a plane. In fact, it was the first time she had ever ventured out of the house on her own. Unable to read and with hardly any practice in speaking English, she miraculously managed to cope with things that we take for granted—using the seat belt and going to the toilet in the plane. When I asked how she managed to transfer to the right plane connection at Melbourne airport for a flight to Tasmania, she blithely told me that she simply followed a Chinese man to his queue, which was actually going to Japan. The kind man showed her to the correct queue.

I was also impressed by her social adaptability; my Western friends and she shared mutual enjoyment and companionship. They informed me that she "spoke quite good English," which I did not have the privilege of witnessing; somehow, mother clammed shut in my presence. She did not clam shut when it came to relishing cheese and cream though. Perhaps the lack of Chinese foodstuffs in Australia in those days became a helpful impetus to her conformity. She had a prodigious zest for living—the first time she encountered snow, she shouted out to me that the lawn was coated with icing sugar. Snow was a meaningless term to her until then. She had sprinted out of the house, sat on the snow, scooping it up with childlike glee, and then dashed back into the house with the speed of a missile.

Though not Chinese-educated, I had always enjoyed the poetic cadences of father's quotations from wise Sages of the past. Indeed, our parents were a living example of what Confucius had propounded—

"If a ruler himself is upright all will go well without orders. But if he himself is not upright even though he gives orders they will not be obeyed."[*2]

The Sage was certainly too idealistic here.

The social structure in the Chinese world shaped by Confucius comprises different relationships. Of the innumerable relationships, Confucius focused on these five, three of which concern the family:

The relationship between ruler and subject;
between father and son;
between husband and wife;
between older brother and younger brother;. All younger siblings have to address their older siblings as 'Big brother, Big sister', etc. between older friend and younger friend.

This leads on to the following attitudes:

Love in the father; filial piety in the son.
Gentility in the older brother; humility and respect in the younger.
Righteous behaviour in the husband; obedience in the wife.

Humane consideration in elders; deference in juniors.
(An older person's point of view is to be accepted politely.)
Benevolence in rulers; loyalty in subjects.

The picture emerges of a society where the family is of eminent importance. In a traditional Chinese family, the father is the head, with the sons taking their place within the family according to their age. The eldest son would naturally step into the role of the demised father. However, the widow matriarch would often take precedence in the family hierarchy over the eldest son, who, in keeping with filial piety would be expected to defer to his elderly mother. One of the most powerful and notorious women in Chinese History, the Empress Dowager, Cixi, (1826-1908) usurped the throne from her son, the Emperor and accelerated the downfall of a proud Empire.

This demonstrates to me a possible crossover of authority between the sexes when it comes to the matter of filial piety. Cixi, a strong woman had unlimited power over her son, the Emperor.

The female sex seemed to count for nothing in the eyes of Confucius. The role of a woman seemed to be confined only to her duty towards her husband and family. What Confucius had to say about women was something as elevating as:

"The only virtuous woman is an uneducated one."

Maybe he was wise and right after all? Should the educated women of today be held responsible for the emasculation of men?

Women feature much in Chinese history and stories. *The Clever Wife* (from the Han Dynasty (206BC-220AD) is an example of an illiterate housewife who, for all her fame was the property of her husband.

Fu-hsing was a lucky man whose wife was so matchless in wit and cleverness that he felt the need to show the world this treasured property. So he inscribed his praise of her on two scrolls displayed at the gate of the house—

"The incomparable wit of Fu-hsing
With ease will accomplish a million things."

Unfortunately one day, a magistrate passing by was offended by this boast. A summons was forthwith sent to Fu-hsing to present himself at court. Fu-hsing shivered and shook in such despair that he was in danger of tearing out the last tuft of his sparse hair as he cried to his wife for help.

"Husband!" his wife put a reassuring arm on his shoulder and said:

"Just go with the magistrate clerk to report to His Worship. We'll discuss the matter on your return. Sometimes the answer is right before your eyes."

Fu-hsing was soon kow-towing to the august presence behind the table with its ink-well and fearsome whip.

"So you are the lowly windbag who dares to boast about your prodigious talent!" His bushy eyebrows crinkled together like two caterpillars locked in fearsome combat. He lifted the awesome magisterial marble slab and crashed it on the table—KLUNK!

"First! I command you to weave a piece of cloth as long as the road!" The first klunk was enough to cause Fu-hsing's vertebrae to disintegrate.

"Second!" KLUNK! KLUNK! "I command you to make as much wine as there is water in the ocean!" There was a painful conk when Fu-sing's head crashed to the ground— he had keeled over from his kneeling position.

Third! KLUNK! KLUNK! KLUNK! "I want you to raise a pig as large as the mountain!" By this time, Fu-hsing believed he was in the Underworld. And the magistrate wagged his fat finger at the now prostrate Fu-hsing.

"You'll see how the court deals with lowly imbeciles like you if you can't carry out my command!"

By the time Fu-hsing had tottered his way home, he had barely any energy to splutter the story to his wife.

"Husband! Oh Husband! There is really nothing to worry about. The answer is simple! Don't you worry your head about it!"

She advised him to present himself in court the next day. All he needed to do was to present to the court the items she had prepared for him and he must remember to say the exact words.

Next morning, Fu-hsing presented himself at court with a ruler, a measuring bowl and a scale. The magistrate's eyebrows were as knotted as before and his face was as ominous as the heavy thunder clouds before a storm

After the mandatory kow-tows Fu-hsing said:

"Your Worship! This morning as I, your useless slave, was hoping to commence the task your Worship has set for me, I realised that I have to humbly beg your Worship for further instruction. Your humble slave therefore has taken the liberty of bringing along these three measures to carry out the task. Your slave respectfully asks your Worship to measure the road with this ruler so that this useless slave can know the length of the cloth. Second, your slave humbly asks your Worship to measure the ocean water with this bowl so as to know how much wine is required. Third, your humble slave begs to know how big a pig to raise after your Worship has weighed the mountain with this balance."

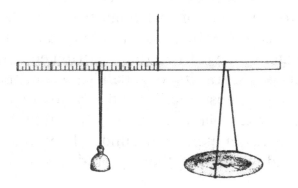

The caterpillars of the magistrate's eyebrows had disentangled themselves entirely and shot upwards by the time Fu-hsing had made his request. The heavy thunder clouds had dispersed as well.

"Your useless slave will be pleased to begin the task as soon as your Worship has set the standards," Fu-hsing announced as he made his deferential bow. When he finally strode out of court, he thought he had emerged through the mist that had been curling about the huge mountain peak.

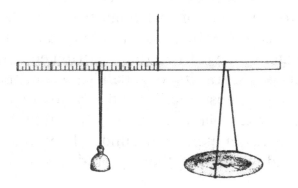

If having to live up to the traditional Chinese expectation of a dutiful wife could be a nightmare, to be married to Confucius must be an act of insanity. Life for Confucius' wife must have been so overly unbearable that she decided to leave him. This was one allegation; however, there exists another allegation that Confucius "divorced" her.

This venerable Sage whose name is synonymous with all Chinese wisdom, was believed to be a person not devoid of human frailties. He was a very difficult person to live with—he was fussy and meticulous in most things. He made great demands on his wife who had to produce food and wines in the special way that only he could approve of. Ginger was not allowed at all in any of his dishes; all foods had to be freshly cooked and the rice had to be "just right". Meat had to be cut precisely to size . . . .

There is a paucity of information about the historical figure of Confucius. He was known to be a scholar who travelled from state to state in search of employment trying to convince emperors of their moral responsibilities to their people. *The Analects,* also known as "the Sayings" or "Conversations of Confucius" is a record of Confucius' answers to a variety of questions from his disciples on various subjects. Confucius acknowledged that he was not the originator of the entire wisdom attributed to him—that he himself had learnt it from the Classics of the past; he was only the "transmitter" of "the Sages of Old." Seen as the perfect teacher who shaped the Middle Kingdom, Confucius was a person around whom his admiring disciples had woven a mythology of idealism.

Although Confucius' teaching stresses the belief in the ideal in man, the female person has not seemed to be worth a mention. Before we have a brief peek at how a female is depicted in Chinese characters, we may need to understand that the Chinese written characters are very complex. A dot or stroke at the wrong place in a Chinese character can bring about a drastic change in meaning. Chinese writing was invented about 4,000 years ago. It is generally believed that there are at least 40,000 characters and 214 radicals. Richard Newnham in his book *About Chinese* (pub. Penguin Books 1971) mentions that the largest Chinese dictionary is alleged to include about 56,000 characters many of which are archaic. The conservative belief is that one needs a minimum of 2000 characters to get a fair grasp of the newspaper or a piece of modern prose literature; and at least 6000 characters to understand technical or classical writing.

The following example illustrates how the components of a character provide clues to its meaning. Chinese characters began as ideograms, signs representing ideas. 女 is an ideogram. When used independently by itself, it stands for "female". The ideogram ⼧ "roof", when combined with another ideogram becomes what is known as a "specifier", or "radical", the part which gives a clue to the meaning of the resulting composite character.

So 女 "female" under ⼧ the "roof" radical becomes 安 a new character, meaning "tranquility" or "security". This character, a woman under a roof, seems to be rooted in the Confucian world of male dominance—the only place for a woman was in the house, to be immersed in housework and bringing up children. Not surprisingly, it also stands for "peace" the precursor to the harmony which will eventuate when the two sexes adhere to their respective roles in society. Confucius' teaching emphasizes individual responsibility and respective roles as mandatory for law and order in the world. When peace is established in the home, it will spread to the community, then to the state, progressing to the country and further afield into the traditional Chinese world. It follows naturally that it is the role of the daughter to be trained accordingly, which of course includes total subservience to her parents-in-law as well as her husband.

As if this is not enough burden on the female, quite a number of Chinese characters connoting negative or evil qualities contain the "female" ideogram.

Below is a short list of such characters with negative connotations containing the "female" ideogram in the role of "specifier" or "radical"

Jealousy 嫉 ji	anger 怒 nu
Slave 奴 nu	hatred 嫌 xian
Demon 妖 yao	stupidity 妄 wang

Let's have a look at what my father had expected of his daughters. He had expected the traditional female virtues, which included chastity, obedience, humility, subservience, cleanliness and industry . . .

A famous book *Admonishments for Girls* written by Bao Zhao (c45-116) on instructions for girls in the palace highlighted three important virtues a woman should possess. These were Humility, Industry and "Enduring sacrifice." I quote:

"Humility means yielding and acting respectful, putting others first and oneself last, never mentioning one's own good deeds or denying one's own faults, enduring insults and bearing with mistreatment, all with due trepidation. Industrousness (sic) means going to bed late, getting up early, never shirking work morning or night, never refusing to take on domestic work, and completing everything that needs to be done neatly and carefully. Continuing the sacrifices means serving one's husband-master with appropriate demeanour, keeping oneself clean and pure, never joking or laughing, and preparing pure wine and food to offer to the ancestors. There has never been a woman who had these three traits and yet ruined her reputation or fell into disgrace. On the other hand, if a woman lacks these three traits, she will have no name to preserve and will not be able to avoid shame."*3

Poor father! Poor us, girls! My painful moan of despair did succeed in extracting a concession from father—yes, I was allowed to laugh but must not show my teeth in doing so. I must purse my lips and laugh demurely behind a handkerchief or a fan. It is interesting to note that some of my Chinese contemporaries today do snigger and cover their mouths with their hands. I wish they would let out a hearty guffaw now and again if only to lend me support!

Father had nursed the fond hope that he would live up to the Sage's expectation and produce children he could be proud of—the boys to be worthy of being the superior male and the daughters to be docile and perfect home-makers. It is amusing to me that after all this weighty expectation of a female, a daughter in a family is normally addressed by non-family members as "Thousand Gold".

Alas! The cultural clashes between us children and our parents had been many. One such epic drama could be traced to this disgraceful eldest daughter whom father had been grooming to be a traditional docile, demure lady of feminine accomplishment, worthy of a place in the exclusive marriage market. This aberration of the Honourable Middle Kingdom had considered embroidery and needlework a laughing matter. This disgraceful being had churned out food that even the family pet had been wary of. In short, this "Thousand Gold" had brought dishonour to the House of Lee by being shamelessly involved in bribery and corruption. She had blatantly operated an essay-writing agency in her sewing class in school, in return for her pals' sewing service. This was made possible because sewing lessons were informal sessions. Our sewing class had always been a happy occasion—the classroom spilled onto the verandah and students were allowed to group around on the floor or anywhere in the classroom in a happy hum of relaxed activity.

You have to believe me that I had not planned to be such a painful disappointment to my parents. It is a marvel to me that they had continued to hold me in such deep affection—even when they nearly expired on discovering that that their hoped-for-delicate-rose of a daughter had turned out to be a bikie at age nineteen!

All right! I am exaggerating! I use the word "bikie" just for effect you know. I did not ride an army-tank of a bike—I had a Vespa scooter. It emitted a pathetic "phut-phut" as I rode down the road and that had the magic effect of alerting motorists to keep a respectful distance from me. I don't believe that this was because they were awe-struck by the distinctive two-tone grey and pink colour of the scooter; rather, it was from a primitive sense of avoiding an accident at any cost.

Owning that Vespa scooter, my own means of transport had brought upon me unexpected attention This "Thousand Gold" of a traditional father had been so focussed on time-saving that she became as sensitive as an elephant's hide. She had no idea what stress she had brought upon her hapless parents. The public transport system had been woefully inadequate and had the nasty habit of gouging big chunks out of her active life. It was, moreover, the painful humiliation of being pummelled and elbowed by fellow passengers that decided her to get rid of the frustration once and for all. Queuing up for service seemed to be unknown in those days and the sight of a strong, young man sitting blissfully oblivious to the fact that it would be humane to give up his seat to a pregnant lady or an old person seemed to cause her unwanted stressful annoyance.

That the State Vespa Club had regarded this disgraceful Chinese daughter as a high-profile member and made a big fuss about her should be seen in the social context of that time. In the 1950's I was only the second female to be seen riding a scooter. I had long become blasé to public ogling, being too absorbed in speeding to meet deadlines.

I was wrapped in my own little world. Even a rude awakening one day did not alert me to the worries and pains that my parents had to endure—they were always restless when I was out on the scooter. On this day, home was within reach—our house was located at the T junction, right behind a set of traffic lights which had just switched from red to green. Normally the familiar "phut-phut-phut" would bring my relieved parents to the door. This time it treated them instead to a rare spectacle—a tangled mass of six men wrapped round their bicycles surrounding my scooter. All this kafuffle had been caused by a loud "Look! Look! A girl riding a motor bike!" from one of the cyclists. The sickening screeching of brakes of my scooter and the vehicles behind me managed to flush out many shoppers seemingly from nowhere. No-one was hurt; the only casualties were my parents who were in a state of near collapse.

This "Thousand Gold" had brought double dishonour to the House of Lee by not only riding the scooter in her rather short pair of shorts, but she seemed to be the first girl to be phutting around with a horde of happy young men at times. The Scooter Club relished the envy of other clubs which failed to attract female members. It never occurred to me how thoughtless and selfish I had been towards my parents. The saying "Youth is wasted on the young" was just so true in this case. Dryden in *The Hind and the Panther* had this for me:

"My thoughtless youth was winged with vain desires . . ."

And what did our revered Confucius have to say about women such as me? Since women were hardly worthy of mention except in their wifely roles, I was, in short, beyond help!

The challenge we face today is monumental. Youth of any era can be insensitive and selfish. In the tidal wave of change it is always the "oldies" who are left to flounder, to come to grips with the inevitable. They would do best to relax in the current of change and go with the flow . . . The struggle to walk up the down-escalator in the peak hour rush is futile—the evolution of change makes it so. As always, it is the wisdom of age that gives that wholesome boost to resilience.

As children we had been helplessly swept along the peak-hour down-escalator. Our world in school and that at home were starkly different. Our parents had a raw deal as well. If that was a heavy cross to bear, then my heart goes out to the perplexed traditional older generations in present-day China and in some other developing countries which are in a remorseless hurry to catch up with the modern world. The challenge of having to face the formidable force of electronic advancement must be quite a strain. Television and the Computer Age have created an enormous divide not only for a government forced to grapple with the concepts of Democracy and Human Rights but also on the hapless parents. The generation gap between parents and children is all the more challenging when the erosion of cultural and moral values can be a cause for pain and puzzlement.

I have unspeakable compassion for the bewildered, illiterate parents in remote villages in present-day China which features two awesomely different worlds—urban China, the world of extreme high tech and that of Old China, in the remote villages caught in a time warp. The helpless poor families in the remote, "last century" world have to face the exodus of their children to the cities, in search of a "better" future. Many of these young people slave away to send part of their wages home to their families. But if the media is a mirror of reality, then they are caught in a horrendous scenario. Girls and women who have experienced the repression of the Old China are becoming drunk with a sense of freedom of choice which they have difficulty handling. The media are largely to be blamed for this. These young girls (and boys) in the spirit of trendy living that the TV and the

Internet portray believe that they have missed out on much and are in a great hurry to make up for lost time. Pub-crawling and seat-warming at Youth cafes are seen as offering a pathway to "modern living". Peer pressure has popularized promiscuity.

Far from the draconian puritanism of their grandparents' world in which the loss of one's virginity could court instant death, some young girls of today's westernized urban China believe that an accumulation of "one-night stands" is trendy—and they would wear that medal with pride. One girl interviewed on television proudly declared that since there is equality of the sexes, "if the boys are bad, we girls, too, can be bad." Looks like "Girls Behaving Badly" is the popular flavour of the day! The bewilderment and sense of loss experienced by the naïve and hapless parents of a "very old-fashioned century" back home in their remote villages seems to be overwhelming. Their faces etched with bewildered pain and losses tug at one's heartstrings.

To the youth of today's world, my parents' world would appear to be as alien as that of another planet. Faithful to a fast, out-moded tradition, my parents, as would their contemporaries, had an uphill climb to maintain their equilibrium in their alien environment. My parents resorted to learning to be patient. "Patience is the companion of wisdom"—St Augustine was absolutely right about this! Our parents wisely accepted that they, too, needed to adapt and teach by example our roles and duties to home and society. They did not forget to add a good dose of discipline, which they believed was the mandatory fertilizer to produce an ordered world.

Always quoting from Confucius, father chanted again:

"Confucius said: "Lead the people by laws and regulate them by penalties, and the people will try to keep out of jail, but will have no sense of shame. Lead the people by virtue and restrain them by rules of decorum, and the people will have a sense of shame, and moreover will become good.""[*4]

The shame factor seems to be of vital importance to the Chinese. To avoid "shame", another term for "losing face" a family would borrow to have a lavish wedding and starve in private.

Confucius did stress that it was the duty of the husband to consult his wife in all matters; a practice my father was very proud of adopting. This had been an easy ride for him because mother with her trust and faith in her husband was inclined to fall in with his suggestions and advice on most occasions. In her marriage to a confident intellectual, mother found this second phase of her life as sheltered a cocoon as her first. Her friends in her childhood days were limited to her siblings and I often had the feeling that when she finally found herself in the wonderland of a life relatively free from the abject poverty of the past, mother was intoxicated with a new lease of life and the discovery of friendship. She loved making people happy. Her generosity was monumental, and often, our unmonumental purse had the remarkable habit of losing weight at an alarming speed. For the same reason, she would joyfully empty her purse to see to her children's every need.

Both of my parents held the belief that the family bond was important and this had been built on a firm foundation of mutual love, respect, trust and an adherence to one's respective position in life. The Chinese have always upheld the principle of respect, especially respect towards elders. Filial piety is sacrosanct in the Confucian world. The Chinese believe that as long as the young respect those older than themselves, especially their parents and teachers, then, that is a first step towards a less chaotic world.

In the Chinese world of my parents, no-one was ever ashamed of growing old. It was taken for granted that just as the parents have sacrificed to give their offspring the best they could afford, it became accepted as a matter of course for these very "offspring"—even when married with families of their own, to return the compliment to their aged parents. The tradition of the extended family had facilitated this of course. It is fair too, to recognise that, with the need for a two-income family and with the stress of modern living, the situation could become very challenging without the support of a robust social welfare system for the old and derelict.

However! It does appear that there is still a cultural divide between East and West on this issue. In the Western world, it seems to be taken as a matter of course that once the children have completed their education, they leave home and their aging parents are left to live independently on their own. A Chinese would often wonder if this eventuates simply because Western aged parents have a fear of impingement on their children. For the Chinese, this brand of pride is not part of the equation. Growing old is accepted as a natural process and embarrassment has no place in this natural course. Ill health has to be cared for with affection—Yes, filial piety is in action here. Each aged parent's birthday is celebrated with sincere congratulations. To live to be a hundred is something the family is proud of. I suppose the Queen of England or the President of USA is doing the right thing here.

But alas! The younger generation in China today, (especially the middle-class urbanites) have seen fit to adopt the trend toward the nuclear family. It seems to be a badge of pride and "modernity" for these people to strike out on their own. Modernisation is synonymous with Westernisation in their perception. This has serious repercussions on the old ones when there is no social welfare in place.

I remember vividly when I was a child coming across a page in my primary reader with a picture of a little crow standing on the edge of a nest with a piece of food for a big crow in the nest. The text was about the baby crow feeding its parent. It read: "Mother crow fed baby crow when baby was helpless. Now, baby crow feeds mother crow when she is helpless." It also read: "Even a crow, one of the less attractive birds, knows it is his turn to look after his old, helpless parent." This had made a powerful impression on me.

Another pictorial story for children went like this: A child eating his dinner at the dining table asked his parents why his granny had to eat hers on a stool in the kitchen. The answer was that she was old. The child dutifully piped up: "When you are old, I shall have a stool for you in the kitchen too." The granny had her meal at the dining table with the family from then on.

Education has its important role in all ages, naturally. It has been recognised that education is not only to impart knowledge and enrich the intellect; it is where character-training and discipline of students' morals and emotions take place. The Confucian ideal conferred great honour upon the educated class. Every family would aim for at least one of its sons to become a Mandarin—to belong to the literati class who had the honour of serving the Emperor. Mencius, a student of Confucius, said:

"Great men have their proper business and little men have their proper business . . . Some labour with their minds, and some labour with their strength. Those who labour with their minds govern others; those who labour with their strength are governed by others. Those who are governed by others support them; those who govern others are supported by them. This is a principle universally recognized."*5

Teachers regarded as literary persons in society were highly respected in the traditional Chinese world. This status symbol vied with that of the medical doctor in the eyes of my father. He held a special reverence for doctors and his special hope was that some of his children would be able to "give their lives" to save lives. He had the wise perception to accept that his cowardly eldest daughter would never fulfil his cherished dream. Without any hesitation, I had to be a teacher. Father cheerfully reminded me that teachers would always be highly esteemed in society. "You see, even an Emperor has to bow to his teacher."

I can see the wisdom of this—it all comes back to the question of respect again. Today's education system could benefit greatly if there were greater respect for the teaching profession and parents could play a vital role in this. Finland has often taken the first prize where education success is concerned. This is mainly due to the fact that the teaching profession is deemed worthy of respect—by students, by parents, and by society at large. Their teachers are well-qualified, the students' aim in school is serious study and the teaching profession attracts dedicated and well-trained people because their salary is attractive. China comes a close second.

The digital age with all its wonderful gadgets is a virtual wonderland compared with the ancient world of Confucian idealism. The concept of the "ideal" and "moral man" in Confucius' teaching can sound very foreign, if not quaint, to today's generation. What is now accessible at the tap of a finger is beyond the comprehension of my parents' generation. The youth of today are a savvy class—in their eyes, google and Wikipedia can be more useful than the classroom teachers. These can do their homework for them.

Our social mores have changed with the advent of Democracy, Freedom of speech and choice gives room to some misguided leftist leanings. The visual medium especially, has a profound effect on the impressionable young. Popular dramas depicting the world of drug culture are prolific with scenes of violence, gore and explicit sex richly flavoured with expletives. This has, unfortunately, become part of the cultural diet of some young people. Nothing seems to be left to the imagination any more.

One positive aspect of today's world is that our savvy young children are less timid about speaking their minds knowing that society has become less prudish. I remember the case of a nativity play in church one Christmas which was less holy in spirit but rich in hilarity. The boy chosen to play the inn-keeper had a grudge against "Joseph" the role he had coveted. When Joseph and Mary called at the inn to ask for accommodation, the inn-keeper dutifully said: "No room! F . . . off!"

Oh! I cannot help yearning for the nostalgic yesteryear, for that subtlety in language. How nice it is to be able to insult with a touch of class:

Winston Churchill comes to mind:

When Lady Astor exploded that she would put poison in his coffee if he was her husband, Winston Churchill coolly assured her that he would happily drink the coffee if she was his wife.

Another Churchillian barb to a waitress was his assurance to her that he could be drunk, but then, he would be sober in the morning, whereas she would still remain ugly.

One other favourite of mine is Oscar Wilde (1854-1900) whose prolific witticisms include this: "Some cause happiness wherever they go; others whenever they go."

There are many others of course. Let us see what John Bright (1811-1889)—British radical statesman and orator had to say about someone with a big ego:

"He is a self-made man and he worships his creator."

The poem—Lee-Mei seems to be more erotic than any of the explicit sex scenes so prolific on today's television and numerous novels. Lee-Mei—written by Anonymous 1930—was alleged to be from a Hakka folk-song.

A young man, deeply in love with a nineteen-year-old girl, stood in the sun with a bunch of white roses, hoping to see her passing by. He was invited in for a cup of tea.

> "Her image play-flitting o'er the scented tea.
> I drank it. Now there is part of her in me,
> And naught can take away this dearest thing."[*6]

Drinking the ephemeral reflection of her face in the tea reflects the sexual connotation of ravished possession.

A couple of years back, I came across an obituary in the *Times of London* bemoaning the demise of an old friend, Common Sense who had been with us for many years. He will be remembered for his simple valuable lessons such as that one should live within one's means; why the early bird catches the worm; why life is not always fair; and maybe the fault is mine. Common Sense adopted the wise strategy that adults and not children are in charge.

Common Sense's health had been deteriorating steadily but surely in our time of Enlightenment, Freedom and Democratic Rights. His health took a turn for the worse when well-intentioned but overbearing regulations were adopted. There were reports of a six-year-old boy being charged for sexual harassment when he kissed his classmate; of parents attacking teachers for doing their job—the parents themselves having abdicated their responsibility and duty to discipline their children and to inculcate in them a sense of Civic Consciousness, responsibility and respect. (I have been equally perturbed to realise that some students seem to rule the schools today and have been known to attack their teachers).

Our old friend's health declined further when schools were required to get parental consent to administer sun lotion to students, but could not inform parents when a pregnant student wished to have an abortion; when the shadow of litigation looms ominously dark and has the habit of playing mischievous tricks as in the case of a woman who carelessly spilled some hot coffee on her lap and was promptly awarded a large settlement.

Common Sense choked on his final gasp for life when one was no longer allowed to defend oneself in one's own home because the burglar could sue the owner for assault. Criminals today seem to be better treated than their victims.

Common Sense's family members who preceded him in death included his parents, Truth and Trust, his wife, Discretion, his daughter, Responsibility and his son, Reason.

It was mentioned that few attended his funeral for the prime reason that many did not realise that he was gone. His surviving four stepchildren are:

I know my Rights
I want it Now,
Someone else is at fault,
I am a Victim

This obituary confirms my infirmity—I have often wondered if I was standing on my head or on my feet. Yes, I am truly dazed and confused and know I have plenty to unlearn. I used to believe that a traitor is one who betrays his country and deserves the utmost of punishment. I am wrong! In today's world, 'Traitor' and 'Hero' are synonyms.

These days, it's real cool to be a traitor, baby!

It was on the eve of one ANZAC Day some years back that three teenage girls had sacrificed their cosy sleep by doing their bit for society—they defaced the Shrine of Remembrance in the night to send their anti-war message!! I believe that these street-wise kids knew which side of the Law they were on—they were just below the legal age for prosecution. Moreover, the hungry media would make them instant heroines!

I would suggest that since the system is so adept at spending precious time and dollars investigating their armed forces for accidental killing of civilians in a war zone and dishing out the same treatment to the police who had to resort to shooting in self-defence in extreme circumstances, I hereby recommend that these police be held up for investigation into the callous fright they gave to those three adolescents who have a social conscience. A hot breakfast of bacon and eggs on ANZAC morning to the heroic girls by way of apology would not be out of place.

On this same morning, hundreds of other young people with their families, who had forgone a hot bacon and egg breakfast, were on a dawn expedition too. They were following the bugle call "Lest We Forget" to honour those who had sacrificed their lives for their loved ones, as is the practice of countries all over the world celebrating their own Remembrance Day. It is indeed heart-warming to see that the number of our ANZAC marchers is swelling each year, nice to know that not everyone takes the Leftist view that ANZAC Day should be wiped off the calendar for being a celebration of war.

These marchers do not perceive ANZAC Day as a celebration of war. For many, ANZAC Day is a day to remember with gratitude those who have made Australia a safe place for us today. Indeed, for those whose family members had died in defence of home and country, it is a sacred day to pay tribute to their gallant predecessors and to be exceedingly proud of them. I salute the families who pass this tradition on to the younger generation. I salute these young people who have a sense of family bonding and love.

Australia is and always will be associated with the ideal of mateship and courage so movingly lived out by their predecessors who died far away from home. ANZAC Day is special to me simply because what is engraved in my mind springs to life on this day—the "Digger", who bears the hallmark of a sun-tanned youth with that laconic sense of mischievous humour drenched with a good dose of larrikinism, had chosen to leave family and country to "do the right thing." If the Diggers could whistle and joke in the face of adversity, their gallant female counterparts in their indispensable support roles were a bulwark of strength in their steadfastness to duty. Their comforting

homey presence radiated that hope of homecoming to
beer and BBQs—one day . . . Many never came back.
Those who did return have lived stoically with horrendous
memories of what had happened to their mates and
comrades-in-arms. The few remaining are a whisper away
from vanishing from our midst forever. Let us never forget
them!

The ANZAC tradition of gallantry and mateship lives
on today, in our men and women in the war zones.
This tradition and Aussie spirit endures simply because
an Aussie is an Aussie and Aussies will appear to give
and help selflessly in times of crisis. Be it a bushfire, a
flood, or a search for a missing person, the volunteers are
there—the friendly, generous Australians will be there
because they are descendants of the Diggers bonded
with the blood-tie of "one for all and all for one." This
fortunately, is a universal trait—we have witnessed again
and again the selfless giving and risking of one's life to
help total strangers in times of war and disaster. At such a
time, it is the spirit of oneness that bonds the victims and
rescuers.

This traditional day of remembrance will further strengthen
family ties and of course, in the Confucius equation, this
will contribute to forging a strong, stable nation. Culture-
rich Australia is so because the United Nations smorgasbord
of immigrants have not only followed the beacon of
"Australia—The Lucky Country"; they know they are
coming to the country of "A fair go for all" welded with a
strong sense of Mateship.

In aiming to pay tribute to my parents and their contemporaries who had faced tribulations and starvation, this book also celebrates the resilience and sacrifices of all who went before me. Our forefathers had blazed the trail with guts and stoicism; this legend has lit the way for the many men and women of today who give of themselves so selflessly, cheerfully and courageously at all times.

CHAPTER 10

DOES A ROSE BY ANY NAME
STILL SMELL AS SWEET?

Since a sense of History was very important to father, the matter of genealogy was therefore of significance to him as it is to all the Chinese. This could derive from the historical fact that the parent-child relationship was the line from which Kingship derived. Keeping the surname down the generations rested on the male heir. Filial piety closely associated with this became the cardinal principle in the Chinese family. Since father was the eldest son in the family, he therefore, had the responsibility of keeping the family tree alive. He was the one who played a vital role in the choice of names for the rest of his male siblings' children. The surname of the family is indeed, a family treasure—it was an inheritance which dated back to the 2nd century BC, after the unification of China. Prior to that period, only the aristocratic class was allowed the privilege of having surnames.

It is alleged that as early as the Han Dynasty (206BC-220AD) each clan in China held a meeting of its leaders to select a list of names for the clan generation names. Today, when a son is born, a father can access to the clan association to ascertain the appropriate generation name. "Members of the Khoo Family Association of Cannon Square in Penang (W. Malaysia) can provide a printed list of the generation names from the 8th to the 47th generation) from their associations."[*1] Many Family Clan Associations and Clan Temples have become heritage centres all over S.E. Asia and China. The value of the daughter in the family pales into insignificance from the mere fact that she stands to lose the family name when she marries. Her surname is unceremoniously replaced by that of her husband's, whose family takes precedence over hers. If her father's and father-in-law's funerals happened to be on the same day, her priority is to attend to her father-in-law's funeral rites at the expense of her own father's. For this obligatory sacrifice, a daughter is labelled "useless" throughout the centuries. Poor long-suffering women! Recent Communist Chinese Government one-child policy has highlighted this fact—every Chinese family would prefer to have a son instead of a daughter and some families have gone to the extreme of cruel disposal of female babies in keeping with the draconian Government policy.

There are three components to a Chinese name—the surname always comes first. Bill Smith in the Chinese context would be addressed as Smith Bill. This is so for the simple reason that the individual is always regarded as of secondary importance to the family. The list of Chinese surnames is very extensive; it could originally adopt a dynastic designation such as TANG—as of the Tang Dynasty (618-906AD), or that of a feudal territory down to that of an occupation or trade. One of the early LEE ancestors was a historical personage, so father told us.

I remember father's fond mention of the fact that our grandfather was a herbal "doctor" with a home-practice. This form of "unregistered medical practice" was and still is quite a common feature in S.E. Asia as well. Unfortunately some of these are labelled as "Quack doctors" by those who have more faith in Western medication. "After all," father continued, "it was only natural that your grandpa was adept at procuring herbal cures for his patients because one of our ancestors was a historical figure who had contributed much in the field of herbal medicine." I did not remember this Mr Lee's full name then, all that I remembered of this famous ancestor was the abiding image of a man who wandered far and wide in search of herbal plants . . . The listening child's mind was really occupied somewhere else—"What if this illustrious man stepped on a venomous snake?"

My research later in life, however, brought me to Li-Shizen 李時珍 (1518-1593). LI is the Chinese pinyin spelling for LEE. Li-Shizen was born in Qichun in Hubei Province and became China's most noted herbalist. Both Mr Lee's father and grandfather were herbal doctors. China's interest in herbal healing and therapy began to take shape as early as the 2nd Century AD. Mr Lee was noted for travelling far and wide to identify the subjects of his research—herbs and plants. The massive compilation of his scholarly research became known as *Bencao Gungmu* or *An Outline of Matria Medica* in translation. The book is divided into six sections, contains fifty-two scrolls and 1160 hand-drawn diagrams as illustration. This entire classic is purported to "contain 1,900,000 Chinese ideograms and list of 1,892 herbs, of which 374 the author added himself. Also included in this classic are 11,096 herbal formulas which was the quadruple of what had previously been written by other authors . . ."*2

It is alleged that many of these formula are considered of great value today. Li-Shizen's interest stretched beyond the study of herbs and plants—his interest in the component of nature encompassed a wide repertoire of topics which included botany, zoology, mineralogy, metallurgy, astronomy and geography. So his *Bencao Gangmu* is more than a pharmacopoeia to the Chinese world. This classic, the result of his 40-year research was considered the greatest scientific achievement in the Ming era (1368-1644) and has been frequently reprinted through the Centuries. Five of its original editions still exist today.

The Li-Shizen award is given to doctors and researchers who have made valuable contributions to traditional Chinese medicines. There is even a Li-Shizen brand of medicine. His medical scholarship and output has not only raised him to the status of Leonardo da Vinci, but has also led him to be compared to Shenmong—a mythical Chinese god known for his instruction on agriculture and herbal medicine. Statues erected in Li Shizen's honour in China depict a reverend scholar attended by a crane—a bird which symbolises long life.

Chinese names usually comprise three characters. Take the example of my eldest brother's name 李鵬展 Li Pengzhan; the second character 鵬 peng following the surname 李 Li, (Lee) would usually be the generation name—in short, males of the same generation have identical elements in this second name <u>though it could</u>

sometimes serve as the personal name instead. This naturally often causes confusion. However, in our Lee family the second name 鵬 peng spans the entire generation of all the brothers and male cousins of the same line.

In our family, the personal name happens to be the THIRD character of the three-character name. 展 zhan is the personal name of my first brother. The Chinese are very assiduous in choosing names which are considered to be character-building. In the case of my brothers, the generation name AND the personal names refer to ideal male characteristics. The generation name 鵬 peng is the name of a huge bird similar to the roc whose huge wing span connotes the ability of the name-bearer to be a protective and responsible person—"all will be safe under his wings," father announced. In the eldest son's personal name, 展 zhan, the third character, literally means "development", so his full name means "great development"—the unfailing ability to protect and care for his entire family and to enhance development throughout his life.

The second son's name is 李鵬程 Li Pengcheng. 程 cheng, the THIRD character, his personal name, means 'career'; so his full name means 'great career'. It suggests the same—he will provide protection for those under his care throughout the journey of life. Unfortunately, three other boys born after this second brother died at infancy.

As if this were not enough to assimilate, my third surviving brother's name which was 李貴鵬 Li Guipeng had the REVERSE order. The second generic name 鵬,

Peng had changed places with the third character, 貴 Gui—"precious". This came about because of father's superstitious need to "save" this third surviving son. He felt that since the three boys preceding the birth of this son had not survived, the seemingly "inauspicious" placing of the generic name had to be rectified—it was moved to the third place. Yes, this third son survived. He passed away in 1996. His name meant "Precious (big) bird" with the expansive wings. He too, would protect those under his wing—firstly the family, then the state, then the country and last but not least "all under Heaven"—the world. In the Confucian context, the family is a microcosm of the world. By now, you are perhaps in such a tangled state of confusion that you consider yourself lucky to have not been saddled with such a responsibility as my traditional father.

If the joy of having a male heir compensates for the challenging tedium of creating an idealized name for a father's precious "bundle of joy", what effort should one put into the choice of a name for that "bundle of disappointment", a "useless" daughter? Most parents perhaps, to assuage their guilty disappointment, are quite happy with the convenient choice of a flower or bird for a name. So names such as "Glorious Rose" or "Lotus Blossom" do bloom away quite happily. Other more comforting names such as "Precious Jade", "Golden Pearl" or "Priceless Jewel" also spring to mind.

"No, not me! My daughter must be quite special!" I can visualize that foreboding jutting jaw of my determined father. He had not forgotten the searing pain that scorched his heart when I, his first-born, the "bundle of shame" came howling into this world. To alleviate his pain and sorrow, father sought to console himself by giving me a very masculine name. It still embarrasses me when literate Chinese would gasp at me with: "What? This is your name? This is a manly name! Too ambitious! Too demanding . . ."

The name father gave me is this: 李勝雄 Li Shengxiong. Its literal translation is "Victorious Hero"! Father ahhed and ummed about this name with "You know, it could signify 'Ever Victorious,' 'Surpasses a man's courage and endeavour,' 'Better than a man' . . ." It was so high in idealism that he seemed to have run out of ideas on how to comfort himself when the rest of his daughters piled up. (Three daughters had been given away to his good friends). All of his other remaining daughters in the family, my three younger sisters, have the same names with the THIRD character 雄 Xiong. Father had to resort to this ploy possibly because his spring of creativity had suffered a temporary setback after such an ambitious endeavour, or he was simply just too smart. The only difference is in the second character, the "qualifier". The sister next to me is 李尤雄, Li Youxiong, 尤 "You", meaning "like" (like the eldest daughter). The name of the other sister is 李亦雄 Li Yixiong, 亦 "Yi" means "following", (following the footsteps of her eldest sister). The youngest sister is named 李如 雄 Li Ruxiong; with "Ru" meaning "the same as" (her name would bear the same expectation and idealism as mine). In effect, all of the three younger sisters have the same characteristics attributed to them as were given to me. They are all 勝雄 Shengxiong "victorious heroes" in idealism and successful achievement.

The Chinese are great believers in the idea that names shape and determine the character of the person. In our case, it had been a terrible blow to father's pride and aspirations that he became blind in his early fifties and had not been able to take care of his family. That was the lowest point of our lives. It was fortuitous that I had just completed High School in 1954 and I became a trainee teacher with a pittance of a starting salary before my next sister completed her High School education and became an audit clerk at Peat Marwick in 1961. My brother started his working life as a trainee bank clerk and he too, did his best to contribute towards the family as well. The other siblings were too young to help.

One other sister had selflessly left school to help in the family. As she is the only person who has a high school education in Chinese in our family, she had to become the eyes and ears of father. Her school education was no match for father's requirement—letter-writing and reading time was always a tearful session for this poor sister who had to help father to "read" letters by holding his hand to "write" the invisible characters on the table. It was the reversed order when father had her to write letters on his behalf— father often "wrote" the invisible characters on the table or in the air for her to decipher. The invisible arabesques were often undecipherable and this became a mutual nightmare. If it was a tearful session for my sister, it was indeed a very painful and frustrating session for father as well. I believe hers was also a very heavy cross to bear. Her contribution to the family was certainly invaluable as she was also the main helper to my mother in household chores.

Father had been supporting his other family in China throughout his life. Often a letter from China would send him into a paroxysm of frustration and anger when it requested additional finance. This situation would entail more letter-writing nightmares when he was fast sinking into total blindness. We continued carrying out this financial responsibility even after father's demise. We had never been pestered for financial help but our mother would continue to send only an annual token amount to China during the Chinese New Year season.

To help in the support of a family of nine, it had become necessary for me to give private tuition at home after school. English and Mathematics happened to be the two most important subjects in schools then. I was very lucky to have the privilege of co-teaching with one of my school colleagues. Sylvia Boudville was a born teacher of Mathematics and I simply enjoyed teaching grammar and English Literature with her. We started with one class of ten students in each "class" of two-hour sessions, three days a week. We were soon able to increase to two classes that spilled into the weekends as well. This became possible only after I had graduated from my three-year teacher-training sessions that took place during the weekends. After Father's death, I was lucky to have the opportunity to teach night classes at the St John's College in the weekends to speed up payment of the house loan to my uncle. Our home tuition classes must have been quite well known since about 50% of the students were from other schools. I am deeply indebted to Sylvia for her selfless assistance in my hour of need. She really did not have to burn the midnight oil but she gave of her best because I had needed her assistance to teach Maths. I also have to thank her for her invaluable typing of notes throughout my University career. These notes were a valuable substitute for the text books which I could not afford to buy. "A faithful friend is the medicine of life" (St Matthew (6:16). St Matthew must have Sylvia and another dear friend, Gill Rose in mind. Gill Rose's untiring physical, moral and spiritual support after a life-threatening surgery later in my life did help me to claw my way back to normal living.

Life was not all a hard plod—I had even found time to enjoy sports in the evening and attended Judo classes at night, believing strongly that I needed to have some knowledge in self-defence. This was sorely needed since I enjoyed visiting waterfalls and rainforests unfrequented by tourists. I believed that I should really be quite adept at throwing potential attackers ever since I became the co-instructor of Judo in the Specialist Teachers College. My Judo instructor, alleged to be one of the best in the State was my "attacker" in our Judo lessons. He would always break his falls with an almighty bang which could have crippled me for life. The art of breaking a fall is very demanding which I had yet to master.

My active life had a tragic toll on father—I had been too occupied rushing about to be aware of the fact that life was one long stretch of frustration and loneliness to a person who was gliding fast into total darkness. The selfishness of youth had desensitised me to his sorrow and pain. I had even failed to grasp the poignancy of his remark that the only comfort he found was the licking of his feet by our beloved brown dog. "Puppy" probably did sense that father was trapped in his tunnel of a never-ending darkness—so Puppy gave father the comfort by staying close to him all day. It has been said that youth is a blunder, manhood a struggle and old age, a regret. Everyone seemed to be too absorbed in his own activities. I was even too blasé to take father seriously when he requested me occasionally to get him some sleeping pills to relieve him of his suffering. I clung to the comforting belief (from a research paper I came across) that a person serious about committing suicide was not likely to "advertise" his intention. We breezed past the bowed head of our patient father sitting on his hard-back chair leaning on his walking stick.

> The wind blows out of the gates of the day,
> The wind blows over the lonely of heart,
> And the lonely of heart is withered away.
> (W.B. Yates: *The Land of Heart's Desire*.)

In the early stages of father's blindness, he would anxiously check the deterioration of his eyes by looking down the street. It was a matter of life and death as far as he was concerned. Sadly he would announce ruefully that "the hole" which gave him partial vision was getting smaller and smaller and the mist around the vision was getting thicker an thicker. With a sigh, he would slowly feel his way back to another hard-back chair and rest his chin on the walking stick. Father refused to be persuaded to sit on the more comfortable "guest" cushioned chair. Then, the eternal scrap-scrap-scrap of the dry broad-leaf fan would lightly brush his shirt. The stifling humidity of the Malaysian climate would cause him to keep this going most of the time, day and night.

I don't recall which of his friends had arranged for him to have an eye operation in the public hospital in Singapore. While at the hospital, his only visitor and carer was the daughter of an old friend in whose liquor shop father had been employed as a manager. Father had an assistant shopkeeper. When father's old friend passed away, father, as usual, was the organiser of the funeral rituals and wake; he was also responsible for reading the obituary. Father had carved himself a notch in this esoteric domain which included marriage rites and ceremony and was therefore in demand especially in the Teochew community whenever the occasion arose. The old couple had a son who seemed to be the exact opposite of the daughter. I remember him as being a tall, handsome and arrogant man with an equally handsome and arrogant son. As a child, I used to envy this handsome young son who seemed to wallow in luxurious opulence. He had the latest of fashion, which he took care to flaunt about as flamboyantly as a peacock fanning out his beautiful tail. He was most proudly conscious of being chauffeured about in an ostentatiously big car.

The Chinese network of benevolent associations had always been responsible for helping overseas Chinese in work—often, it was a matter of helping one another. Father had never been short of an appointment, seemingly very versatile and professional in his work ethos. Luck seemed to be on father's side all the time since his employers had always been friends or people who admired him. In short, father never seemed to be in want of employment. It was therefore a rude shock to us when he stormed into the house one day in a state of high agitation. He seemed to be quite ill and announced that he had burst a blood vessel in his eyes. All I remember was that the arrogant son had unwittingly rudely asked the shopkeeper: "Where is that Lee Oon Gam? He should be here, in the shop!" Father happened to hear this. It was not only the peremptory tone of the question, but the contemptuous disrespect due to him who was always addressed as "Uncle" that caused father to storm out of the shop.

He never returned there again. He could not, even if he had wanted to. Father believed that the insult was the cause of his partial loss of eyesight from that day.

That was the cruel beginning to an unfortunate sequel. I remember father saying that he was delighted that the operation in Singapore had been successful. He devoured the daily newspaper hungrily while at the hospital. But alas! What transpired was that on the check-up day, he was being reviewed by a team of internees. I remember father's remark that he was in a room with them and they had trained some optical gadget on him. He lost his eyesight entirely when he left the room. We were living in a simpler world in those days and complaint against an authority and litigation was not a known thing—especially in our naïve, inexperienced family. So father had to face his death sentence as a matter-of-fact sequence. Days merged into nights and with this dark pall, sorrow and despair gnawed deeper and deeper into his system. To alleviate the monotony, father would grope about the house "tidying" what he believed had to be done and shifting chairs silently, slowly, from one place to another.

Insomnia set in and we would sometimes hear the muffled and almost inaudible shuffling sound of movement—father was going about his nocturnal self-imposed task of arranging all our footwear in neat rows. Often, on cool nights, we could feel the sheet gently falling on us. Father had always been a meticulous and caring person. He had always been a man of action; in his spare moments, he would be composing poems which he would use in his speeches or performance of rites.

Nowadays, his fingers would dance and slide on his lap or on the table even when he was supposed to be resting on a chair—he was practising his calligraphy or writing a verse. He had never lost his love of calligraphy. I remember a time when he was able to write calligraphy as small in size and as elegant in nature as the proud imprint on a porcelain bowl.

潮州八邑會館

*3 This is the photo of the Teochew (Chouzhou) Benevolent Association in Kuala Lumpur, where father had served as a committee member.

One highlight that father enjoyed was phone calls from his friends who would ring up periodically for a chat or to ask for some advice. Father seemed to refrain from phoning them for reason that he believed they would be too busy to be interrupted by him. As chirpy and talkative as usual, he was always happily alert when the garden gate creaked— he always nursed the hope that it was a visit from one of his friends. This would be the only occasion when father allowed himself the luxury of sitting on a cushioned guest chair. The minute any of his friends greeted him, father, bubbling with happiness would loudly call out "Tea come!" We would naughtily mimic the order and one of us would be the respectful provider of innumerable cups of tea.

The peak of father's happiness was the one time when there was a fifteen-week one-hour programme at noon on every Monday. It was a rare and beautiful programme in "Teochew" about the love and care of a daughter for her aged father. Like raindrops to a parched land, father drank in greedily the gentle and affectionate voice of the filial daughter. It provided a valuable catharsis to a lonely man who clung to the words he craved from life as desperately as a drowning man clutching at a drift wood in the sea. It was very unfortunate that our family, somehow, were not physically demonstrative, touching each other and saying "I love you," to a family member had never happened; the dwelling place for such affectionate terms were in the heart and in the heart alone. Father seemed to be the only member in the family who could demonstrate his love for his children physically and naturally; but alas! That was our fault—that luxury only existed in our childhood. Teenage years and of course, our teenage active life contributed to our alienation, we were living in a separate world from our father's. I remember, however, that I was the lucky one who seemed to be very close to a demonstrative father till I was thirteen years old. To my wonderment, on my thirteenth birthday, food and wine was laid out for the ancestors. I had to kow tow while father mumbled a speech as was his habit when we prayed to our ancestors. Then father solemnly announced to me that from that day onwards, I was a woman and we should not hold hands again. A woman? I had no idea what he meant. I certainly could not find any difference in me between that day and the day before. Father seriously announced that from that day on, I was mother's responsibility and I should direct all queries and matters to her.

I was lost in a crushing despair. From the "damning" age of thirteen, was I to be deprived of father's company? Was I to be barred from that magic world when we revelled in stories of China's civilisation and exploits of heroes and heroines of a visionary, romantic past? His love for his children was strong and deep; he took great pride in giving us names weighty with idealism and value. Traditional Chinese valued patriotism and deified sons who had given their lives to save their countries. Though traditional China had always devalued the female sex and it had been a habit of families to be disappointed in the birth of a daughter, Chinese history, however, has always paid tribute to women who had outdone men in the course of history. Father's tribute came in the form of tales to his children in celebration of their courage and selfless sacrifices. He revelled in the dramatization of Hua Mulan, (木蘭 means "lily magnolia"). She happened to be the extraordinary female who secretly disguised herself as a male and was celebrated in History as one whose excellence in military art and leadership in war saved her country. The lily magnolia here certainly belied her capability—her military leadership of a vast army. The little girl used to be so inspired by this epic story that she thought she should be given a horse and be a very brave cowgirl to gallop at full speed into the sunset to save the world.

I have never believed that my father really ranked women as useless. The traditional Chinese male chauvinistic attitude in our father had ample room to uphold the ideal that women should never lose their femininity. Indeed, father relished the female charm and sensuality which attributes he recognised could become more powerful than the most powerful emperor in the world. It was in the stories of the femme fatales in Chinese history that father found most gratifying; these were especially poignant when beautiful women used their seductive charm and accomplishment in changing the world for the better. One such national heroine was the famous Wang Zhaojun, known in History as the Lady Diplomat

China's history was a chronicle of warfare with the "barbarians," the nomadic tribes of the desert and steppes beyond the border of China proper. The Han Chinese, noted as the original ethnic group of China lived around the two main rivers, the Yellow River (Huang He)and the Yantze River One of the fiercest of the nomadic tribe was the Xiongnu who had plagued the Empire with bloody incursions and pillages. The Chinese were no match for these marauding attackers mainly because of their ferocity and superb horsemanship. To safeguard China from these periodical onslaughts, Qinshi Huang, the first Emperor (221-207 BC) extended the Great Wall of China. This, however, had not been a successful deterrent. The Celestial Empire would then try to placate the Khans with lavish gifts and offerings of marital relationship with minor princesses from the court.

It was during the reign of Emperor Han Wudi (140-100 BC) that the Xiongnu were beaten back and the Han

Dynasty expanded deep into the Province of Xinjiang. Nevertheless, peace with the nomads was as fragile as in the past. When the Emperor passed away, his son, Han Yuandi ascended the throne and one of the first things he did was to free his father's 3,000 concubines and replaced them with new ones. A concubine appointment could be a first step towards imperial recognition if she could remain the Emperor's favourite and present him with a son. Many concubines faced a tragic fate however. There had been cases of their reaching old age without ever seeing the emperor. The Emperor was often too busy to personally view his choice, so he relied on court portraits of these beauties to make his choice.

At this time in history, there lived a maiden of surpassing beauty, Yuan Zhaojun 怨 昭君, age sixteen, was the daughter of a minor court official. Zhao 昭) meaning "bright", "luminous", "eminent"; and Jun, (君), has a respectful male reference of "lord" or "king", which might be considered an auspicious combination for this noble princess. Women in the elite strata—rich men and nobility class were not only surrounded by grandeur, and riches, they were also pampered with maids in attendance on them day and night. These ladies were generally well-educated in the Confucian Classics and as was the practice in the traditional Western world down to the later time of Jane Austen, genteel women were expected to be educated and well-versed in the arts of embroidery, painting, music and literary contribution. Traditional China adhered to this practice throughout the ages and this had repercussion on the traditional world. Zahojun was not only well-known for her beauty; she was an intelligent girl, well educated in the Confucian Classics, and was well trained in the traditional arts of calligraphy, painting, embroidery, dancing and music. She specialised in playing the pi-pa, an ancient Chinese plucked instrument. It was her famous beauty which unfortunately brought about her undoing—she caught the eye of the imperial scout and was recruited as a court concubine. The Court painter, a Mao Yanshao, was unfortunately a corrupt man who exploited his position with extortions from the concubines whose fate rested on his portrait painting. Zaojun refused to be bribed on principle and the result was an unflattering portrait that the Emperor was presented. This resulted in a life-sentence to the lonely quarters known as "the Cold Palace," where other unfortunate concubines languished for the rest of their lives.

This happened to be the era when the Xiongnu tribe was riddled with internal rivalries and the Khan, Huhan Xie, decided that it was to his advantage to rally the support of the Han Emperor. His homage visit to the Empire had been a great success. It was to the advantage of the Chinese Empire to buy peace with the Khan so Huhan Xie was lavished with precious gifts and the offer of a court concubine for wife.

Concubines cringed at the thought of being driven to this fate. The fear of the unknown was amplified by the stigma of marriage to a "barbarian." No volunteer stepped forward. Zhaojun after weighing her fate in the Cold Palace decided that she might take this opportunity to do something useful in her life and offered herself to the Emperor. The Khan was more than delighted with the vision; while the Han Emperor stupefied by her ravishing beauty regretted that he could not go back on his promise.

The royalties were further astounded by her music and dance. Legend had it that the angry emperor had the corrupt painter executed.

Wan Zhaojun was immediately tutored in the foreign language and state affairs. She assimilated into the nomadic life of horse-riding and hunting and was well accepted by the society. Her private world was a life-long sorrow in her desperate longing for her home country. She would often send gifts and regards to the Emperor at the capital and he would reciprocate in return. In her homesickness, she composed a touching poem which was sung in accompaniment with her favourite instrument, the pi-pa. This famous song known as "the Sorrow of Zhaojun" touched the hearts of the Chinese nation. The lyric has been lost; however, the title has gone down in history as the name of a verse 'ci' (pattern).

Her intelligence and diplomatic handling of the tribe brought about a change—the tribe was encouraged to cultivate the land in lieu of military incursions. The more than sixty years of peace in her lifetime was attributed to her. She produced a son for the Khan, but when he died, Zhaojun was expected to marry the new Khan, her stepson as was the tribal custom. This was against her Confucian principle and she pleaded with the Chinese Emperor for permission to return to China. This plea was rejected. Zhaojun married the stepson and gave him two daughters. It seemed her intelligence and female charm was more powerful than military might in securing peace for her country.

Zhaojun's lonely yearning for her home country lasted till her death in old age. Her request to be buried in the desert at the southernmost border of Inner Mongolia nearest to her native China had been granted. It is said that the area around her tomb was always green with vegetation. It is known as the "Verdant Tomb of Han Princess". Wan Zhaojun was known in history as the Lady Diplomat.

A thin mist veiled father's eyes when he mentioned Zhaojun's yearning for her home country. Father too, had this yearning—it had been his life-long dream to visit his ancestral home and his father's grave. When it transpired that father had never been able to realise his dream, I took it as a commitment to do this on father's behalf but was only able to fulfil this duty in 2001. After father's death, contact with father's daughters in China had been an annual New Year token of a red packet till the demise of mother. The proxy correspondent for father had always been our Chinese-educated sister. I was therefore, most surprised to discover that the families in China did know about me—they had, in fact, a photo of my University graduation, sent, most probably by my mother.

My first port-of-call was Shantou, where given-to-adoption sister lived. My last memory of her was when we were children, before her family moved back to China. I was seven years old and she was five. It was quite a demanding effort for the families in China to get used to my strange accent. My Teochew dialect was certainly not up to their standard. I couldn't appear to be more stupid and slow, every simple conversation we had was a dramatic comedy; their patience towards me was phenomenal. For a start, they found me and my friend from Sydney, Correll Fawcett, rather quaint and they couldn't do enough to make us feel comfortable and welcome, down to the minutest detail such as fighting to peel an orange for us and piling our plates and bowls with the choicest of food.

We were met at the Shantou airport by my biological sister and her family. They had hired a taxi which had to wait for more than an hour for us because our connecting flight had been delayed. We could not fail to miss them— they were the only ones who appeared like a flock of flamingos straining their outstretched necks in anxiety. My first reception from my sister was a flood of tears which caused me much unease, being unfamiliar with emotional demonstration. I found out very soon that she had the memory of an elephant—she remembered every detail of my first and last meeting with her and I was soon acquainted with the sad story of father's last visit to China. She cried piteously that her fate could have changed for the better had she not missed father "by the inch"— returning home from school the moment my father had left the house. It appeared that father's visit had been made awkward because her adopted mother had not welcomed father's offer of an arrangement to take my sister back to our family in Malaysia. Father's offer was meant to be a gesture of assistance since their family situation had not been ideal—they were also facing some financial difficulties.

This sister in China has three children; one boy and two girls. I missed one of her daughters who was working in another city during my visit. It was a delightful family; my poor, sweet brother-in-law who could not speak

English was the perfect "Noddy" with a perpetual smile on his face. Banned from drinking alcohol, he appeared to have full self-control in not being affected when others drank in his company. This was a relief to me and my companion whose habit of wine-drinking at dinner was very gleefully adopted by the other two men in the family—my nephew and nephew-in-law. The family made every effort to show us around; they had borrowed a car from a friend and our daily outings must be a rare treat to those who could be party to a sardine-packed car of six. This means of transport made it possible for us to spend a day at Chaozhou where I had the privilege of visiting our ancestral home.

It was indeed a very special day for all of us. My father had two daughters; the eldest surviving daughter was blind. I envied her poetic eloquence—she was only twelve years younger than my mother; unfortunately her blindness seemed to add years to her age and I had difficulties addressing her as "Sister"—she seemed an old granny to me. Everyone was most polite and hospitable. A car had been organised to show us around after lunch. We were treated to an impressive lunch at an opulent restaurant where every member of the diners was formally introduced to me. I felt quite comically awkward when young and old kept bowing and addressing me as "Aunty" and "Grand aunty". It was a little difficult for me to keep a straight face when some of father's grandsons seemed to be about fifty years old. Being delegated to the VIP table was only the beginning of an unusual day. The lunch had seemed formal except that everyone seemed to compete to fill our plates with all the choicest of food. I was a rich source of entertainment and possibly embarrassment as well.

No wonder father had labelled his family in Malaysia as barbarians. I seemed to be an odd creature for not using the chopsticks to shuffle rice into my mouth and horror of horrors! I, their grandaunty was known to guzzle beer and wine with remarkable alacrity.

I did wonder how my parents would have reacted had I recounted the tea session in father's family home. Father's family home was a quaint and dilapidated brick house with a courtyard and well. The front sitting-room of the house spilled into an open courtyard with a small room on each side. The main house had two wings with a bedroom each. The only toilet (a modern flush toilet that had been installed for my blind sister) was at the back of the house adjacent to a small kitchen. What caught my attention was a fairly large gaping hole in the middle of the roof which clearly marked the boundary of the two wings of the house previously occupied by the two sisters, my father's daughters. The only occupants of the building at the time of my visit were my blind sister and her unmarried daughter. Father's younger, deceased daughter's three sons (the fourth son had been unable to take off work for my visit) sat in their wing of the building. At the other wing of the house was my blind sister's family of three daughters and two sons and my brother-in-law who had yet to utter a single word to me on that day. What fuelled my amusement was that both families sat in a straight line facing each other. My friend and I were the centre of attention and everyone continued to compete in the race to offer us fruits, sweetmeat and cup after cup of tea. There was much hilarity (out of politeness, I think,) in every of our utterance. The big drawcard was my camera—we had many photos taken and these rigid, polite people seemed to be well entertained by me, the photographer who was behaving like a grimacing monkey. I was well paid for the effort—the ice was broken, the smiles and hilarity in the photos were charmingly natural.

The fun, for me at least, really started when the heavens opened up and a deluge of water soon took over the open courtyard and the family in the sitting-room had to scramble for safety It was a unique situation that when the downpour stopped as suddenly as it had started, the hosts had to run about to bucket out the water. When the drama was over, it was a formal return to the straight-back chairs to continue with the eloquent and polite conversation, only ten per cent of which managed to percolate through my dense brain. I had difficulties keeping a straight face when the scene of the mad hatters' tea party in *Alice in Wonderland* occupied my mind. When I asked the obvious question why they did not fix the gap in the roof, the answer was the fait-accompli attitude that the Government would need the land for development and the poor owners would have no choice but to accept an alternative offer of housing. This seemed to be the situation of my biological sister. I believe that the standard size apartment on the sixth floor of a high-rise building is an alternative offer from the Government when they had to give up their original property. The prospect of lugging groceries up the interminable winding steps would be a top-class incentive for one to opt for a starvation diet.

The goodbye was another memorable occasion. Our biscuit-tin size of a car had to negotiate a very narrow lane out to the main road. Houses with open doorways and rooms with residents in all varieties of house chores and idlers in various lazy postures stared at us as the biscuit-tin size of our car was making every effort to avoid knocking down pots and pans, furniture, humans and dogs. My relatives, old and young seemed to fall into a guard of honour line exuberantly shaking hands with the amused barbarian aunty from Australia on whom they had lavished local gifts. Father would have been proud of the family's filial piety duty to him. I was shown photos of the family in mourning attire bowing to a portrait of father when they received news of his demise. A headstone in memory of father had also been erected in the family cemetery

Over the years, I have never ceased to regret that I had not plucked up enough courage to say to the bowed head of father: "Pa, my papa! I cannot live up to your glory and aspiration of a wonderful daughter. I am very grateful to you for enriching my life with tales of glory and splendour of the country which language I have no mastery of. I thank you, my papa, for this rich culture and heritage which I shall do my best to share with others. The least I can do now is to teach English in helping to keep the family afloat and I assure you that this is a labour of love. Your contribution to our lives is beyond payment and I shall strive to honour you by becoming a *"hsiu-tsai"* (Flowering Talent) through the University."

CHAPTER 11

EDUCATION AND THE IDEAL MAN

In this chapter, I am straddling two worlds—that of today, the Now, and the other world flavoured with my father's rich cultural heritage. Education trends have died and resurrected in different transformation none more so than now. We are in the midst of rapid evolution of digital marvels. Quo vadis? I can't answer that for the current generation. Let me start with: where do we go from here? How fulfilled are we as individuals in the fast lane of today's digital world? Then I hear my father's lone voice echoing from the void of the other world that stressed that the role of Chinese traditional education is to shape the ideal man—a "civilized" man.

My teaching career in Australia in the '70s landed me in a world of some confusion. It seemed to me that it was only "yesterday" when I entered the classroom in Malaysia, the students stood up for me and remained standing till asked to be seated. They then plodded on with their Grammar exercises and Literature study with interest and seeming enjoyment. "Work hard to compete to be the best" seemed to be the unwritten rule of the day. "Today", the classroom I walked into in Australia was a room of noisy, chatty students who flopped over their desks and continued to engage in loud conversation with total disregard of the presence of the teacher. It took my students sometime to work out what my expectations were. Teaching Matriculation students did help—they were aware that they needed to work to get to university. Albert Einstein's view that the supreme art of the teacher is to awaken joy in knowledge suited me well here. The love of Literature made my teaching of the subject a joyous experience. My dream for my students stretched beyond getting them through the examinations.

It was a challenging time for me though in that period. What gave me a major shock was the trend that "free expression" seemed to be the IN thing. The teaching of Grammar was not accepted as important—the three Rs— "reading, writing and arithmetic" seemed to be dying a near-painful death as well. I remember being elated with the news, in 2009, that 102 teachers from Queensland alone had sacrificed two weeks of their school holiday to attend one of the six ten-day residential course funded by the Federal Government to focus on literacy, numeracy, English, Science and Mathematics. That was the start of a new four-year $102 million programme. A little late perhaps, a generation of grammar-deprived people are still writing and saying things such as "there is fifty people in the room . . . its alright . . ."

It is obvious that not only should teachers be expected to have a solid, proper teacher-training and have a sound knowledge of the subject that they are teaching, but they should also deserve to have a clear-cut national curriculum to work from. The attempt to overhaul the school curriculum in 2011 was tremendous news to me.

It seemed to herald the entrenchment of the teaching of English, Mathematics, Science and History. The latter has suffered the label of "soft option" by students for too long.

Samuel Taylor Coleridge bemoaned the fate of History thus:

"If men could learn from History what lessons it could teach us! But passion and party blind our eyes. And the light which experience gives us is a lantern on the stern, which shines only on the waves behind us."

This seems to echo the traditional Chinese view of the importance of History study.

"He who reads History knows the affairs of the ancients" and we learn from their mistakes.

Yes, what a pity! The value of history stretches beyond learning from our past, it provides the bridge to a sense of belonging to a past heritage that has been meaningful and enduring.

It had been a confusing and lonely time for me from the late '70's onwards, when the trendy practice then was to condemn the teaching of Grammar in English. It seems a strange "phenomenon" that one believes that the teaching of a Foreign Language has to be built on a strong foundation of Grammar which has been accepted as a sound building block towards the understanding of a language, yet this has been argued against when the teaching of the English Language was concerned.

As the years rolled by, education trends of the day seemed more than "passing strange" to me. We have been through the era when education policies were being shaped by trendy technocrats who believed that one of the aims of education was to erase the capitalist system so as to bring about the "socialist" utopia. The three Rs that I was brought up with were replaced by another trio— "Republic, Refugees and Reconciliation." The handful of education bureaucrats brought in new, radical systems one of which was Outcomes-based Education which was to allow students to progress at their own pace. The system was essentially student-based: non-competitive, the focus was on "process," not content; children were free to choose what they liked to read. Teachers were to play a secondary role—they were known as "facilitators."

It was with some trepidation and perplexity that I tried to comprehend how the politically correct agenda of the day would affect the teaching of English/Literature. In the year 2009, the AATE, The Australian Association for the Teaching of English disagreed with the National Curriculum Board's definition of school English as the three elements of English, Literacy and Literature. The AATE did not seem to place a high value on the teaching of literature. Instead, it advocates "meaning-making" in, and through a range of different forms of writing with the media to be recognised as the core organiser of the curriculum. "This other types of English texts" would include films, TV shows, advertising, signage, text messages and web-site.

The whole-language method was advocated. Instead of teaching phonics and phonemic awareness, the argument was that children should "look and guess" at meanings and spellings. "Making meanings" was the buzz term of the day. Grammar and punctuation were not regarded as important; children were to be encouraged to express themselves freely. Teachers' corrections of children's work were deemed to be "intimidating . . . disempowering students' creativity . . ." I presume that the submission of a student's Art Examination paper which was painted entirely in black and titled: "Power Failure" might be lauded for artful free expression.

In this time of revolutionary soul-searching, the impulse of the Cultural Left to free education from the past seems to be influenced by prejudice which regards ideas of the past as old-fashioned and irrelevant. Present education fads tend to flatter children that they are savvier than their parents in this new digital society; and the experiences of yesteryear bear little significance and are irrelevant to their schooling. Curriculum engineers often tend to display indifference, if not contempt, for abstract thought and knowledge developed in the past. The traditional academic curriculum is labelled as obsolete, unsound, socially unjust and competitive.

I wonder if it is outlandish to cling to the fond belief that the purpose of education is to acquire knowledge and a place for scholarship, and that should not be seen as an elitist leaning. It is that very academic standard that enriches one's intellect and enhances one's spirituality. I believe we are lucky to have a past heritage, a treasure house of wisdom and knowledge to draw upon and to learn from. Mr Frank Furedi's article in *The Weekend Australian* 7/8 November, 2009, supported the views of educationists and philosophers that we have a rich cultural heritage which should be preserved. The value of education lies in this transmission of lessons learnt by humanity through the ages, which serve to equip each succeeding generation with the cultural and intellectual resource to deal with the challenge of change. Mr Ferudi also acknowledged that in Anglo-American societies, curriculum planning do take cognizance of the need to cultivate an ethos of flexibility towards the future.

Ex-Prime Minister Kevin Rudd's flamboyant articulation about our students' need to be "information-rich and computer-literate" in order to make big waves in the 21st Century did resonate well with the public at large and did help to get him some votes. It is well recognised that the role of education is more than a computer-literate society working towards a fat salary for life. I am optimistic that there are others out there who recognise the role of human relationship and personal interaction in the enhancement of one's humanness.

The electronic age seems to have given birth to a new culture with its own body of lingo that serves to widen the generation gap—the computer-literate young from the older computer-dummies with their "outmoded" ideas about respect and caring for others. I think the role of education has a little more to it than producing computer hi-tech wizards. Sounds familiar—father's voice? What should be nurtured in our young street-wise generation is that there is something sublime known as love, compassion and sensitivity to Beauty and Goodness all that which generates a sacred respect for life and for another human being. The role of education is to enhance this humanness in an individual, to imbue and enrich the moral, emotional, spiritual and intellectual aspect of our being. Oh yes, my father's voice again, from that other world of Confucian idealism in the human kind and a humane society.

One person I have great respect for is Dr Kevin Donnelly, the Director of Education Standards Institute, author of *Dumbing Down* and *Educating Your Child: It's Not Rocket Science*. His intelligent voice has been bravely strident against the vociferous Leftist elements of the education world. In the article—*Evolution of Education,* in *(The Weekend Australian),* Dr Donnelly touched on a humanist's view of education by referring to an address to the Mont Pelerin Society delivered by David Green, an analyst in the London-based Institute of Economic Affairs. David Green summarised historian Max Hartwell's presentation of a liberal-humanist's view of education as: that education should embrace "civility, morality, objectivity, freedom and creativity." He elaborated that by civility, he meant respect and regard for others; by morality, the basic elements of common decency, honesty and fairness; by objectivity, an unbiased examination of facts and arguments; by freedom, the principle that children should be given the opportunity to appreciate the value of personal responsibility so as to be well prepared to exercise it through life; and by creativity, a belief in the advance of knowledge which leads to the possibility of progress.

How refreshing! Does sound like my father!

Traditional Western Education encompasses a rich literary canon represented by Greek tragedies and philosophies; a rich body of knowledge incorporating aspects of Judeo-Christian tradition and the Great Classics of the ages—all this for the taking, so well enunciated by Matthew Arnold,—poet, and schools inspector in the Nineteenth Century. A liberal education to him was "Getting to know, on all matters which most concern us, the best which has been thought and said."

The Canon of Great Classics enriches us with a three-dimensional view of other worlds and other lives' experiences. Without these, our lives would be sadly impoverished, very empty indeed. It opens to us the magic casement of human matter which is dealt with movingly and with profundity. Its richness of language and power of imageries lift us to the sublime as powerfully and potently as the operas of Verdi, Donizetti . . . the music of Beethoven, Mozart . . . We soar with the magic of words and ride on the wings of music to enter this other world and depths of emotions and to emerge with a more appreciative view of life, after being entranced by the wonderment of man's creativity and resilience in the face of tribulation.

Confucius has ascribed music to be an important component of education in the shaping of a humane and virtuous person. A great musician in his own right, it appeared that he was often so immersed in listening to music that he would forget his meals.

I made my mother cry when she chose to come to live with me in Australia. My illiterate mother who had no previous exposure to any form of Classical music and operas had been a top-class student when it came to appreciation of such wonders. A brief synopsis of an opera was sufficient to induce total immersion in her case.

"Music that knows no country, race or creed;
But gives to each according to his need."

Music, indeed, is an international language.

Mother was indeed, my soul mate. I would be loath to have my children be denied this vision splendid, and be deprived of this feast of words wondrous and splendiferous.

Professor Susan Greenfield's excellent book, *The Quest for Meaning in the 21ˢᵗ Century* has made a great impression on me. She questions what kind of people will the new digital world produce? And how fulfilled would they be? The digital world with its cyber technology is upon us and its tentacles are expanding rapidly, wrapping a generation of people in its relentless grip. It is believed that in the year 2012, one in five persons in the world possessed a digital gadget of some form other. The computer with its Google and Wikipedia are the convenient engines to deliver information often appearing in helpful "bite-size" chunks. Homework to our students is generally a copy-and-paste exercise. Some students might be inclined to exert minimum effort to think, analyse and understand the subject in depth. The social networking of Facebook, Twitter, not to mention blogging, would have a great influence on how young people think. These facilities can and have revolutionised the world.

We have a generation of young people who are so obsessed with IT and cyber technology that they often forego life and exercise in the outdoors to the detriment of their health. Many tend to subsist on a diet of screen culture which opens a world of continuous speedy tumble of thrills and kills in an overload of adrenaline-driven exploits. The hyper stimulation of this virtual world of "second life" introduces a complete new world of alienation from reality. The Buddhist belief that life is only an illusion never seems to hold more true here. It is not difficult to appreciate why these young people find that real life in the family and school is drab and boring. The long span of attention needed in school studies that we of the Twentieth Century are familiar with, has caused the education fraternity big problems. The attention span needed in immersing oneself in a good book and be engaged in the old-fashioned abstract thinking and savouring of the written words is in danger of being obsolete.

One optimistic view is that all this technological magic has produced a generation of savvy young people. They are indeed, information-rich and their social-networking enables them to share and learn from their peers. This certainly suits them very well because parents often are one of the last people to know what is going on in their children's world. IT has revolutionised our 21st century education and thinking. Our classroom teaching methodology needs to change and our teachers with a solid training in IT will be more effective in their profession.

I believe that Britain has been thinking of padding street lampposts to protect pedestrians who are too engrossed in their latest digital gadgets and text messaging to mind their steps. Apologists are quick to point out that at least they are writing and reading. However, text messaging does not encourage one to use a wide vocabulary and indeed, it encourages the abbreviation of spellings and expression. Correct grammar usage is out of place here. This quickie message-making and the popularity of the screen culture has the tendency to strangle the intellectual response to "meaning" and "feeling".

In this Brave New World of ours with the advent of biotechnology, information technology and the invasive nanotechnology, we have come a long way, indeed, from yesteryear. Father would be envious of our medical advancement. He is speechless with amazement, I know.

"The impact of nanotechnology touching, as it will, on every aspect of life from crime prevention to energy conservation, to healthcare is almost too breathtaking and impossible to contemplate."[*1]

On page 253, Professor Greenfield has this from the astronomer Carl Sagan when he contemplated on a world facing the imminent march of technology:

"It is suicide to live in a society dependent on science and technology, where virtually no one knows anything about science and technology."[*2]

Indeed! Our twenty-first century brand of the New World with its limited number of elitist grand masters is fast upon us The focus of Greenfield's book is on the need to examine and study how our minds and thinking interact with the current stream of technological innovations. Only then,

"will we be able to plan the kind of education, as well as the goods and services, which we shall both want and need by the mid-twenty-first century."*3

However, there is a nagging discomfort—What price our privacy? What price our human sensitivity? With the possible availability of cloning and designer babies, where does the great Confucian thinker, Hsun-tzu, (who believed that Man's fundamental nature is bad) stand with this declaration:

"When social statuses are equal (sic), there will not be enough for everybody. When men's power is equal, here will be no (way to achieve) unification and when people are equal, no one will be able to command the services of others . . . Two nobles cannot serve each other, and two humble persons cannot command each other. This is the law of nature. When people's power and position are equal and their likes and dislikes are the same, things will not be sufficient to satisfy everyone, and hence there cannot but be strife. Strife will lead to disorder and disorder will lead to poverty."*4

The essence of the traditional Chinese mind flows towards the concept that man and nature form one society. The universal order is important—and it is not advisable for man to dominate nature with the help of Science. The Daoist spirit is in play here—Man should seek to integrate with nature.

Debates have run riot about the effect of the screen culture and video games and the desensitising of their devotees. Many heated arguments have focussed on the truth and untruth of what research has come up with—that "there are significant short-term and long-term effects of violent content . . ." All the same, it is hard to be complacent about news items on unprovoked youth violence and brutality. One such item dealt with the video game "Grand Theft Auto" (in 2008) which was alleged to have inspired several teenagers on a crime spree according to Nassau County, New York Police. The game portrayed the player stealing cars, killing bystanders, sleeping with prostitutes before killing them.

Professor Susan Greenfield estimated that in Japan, (in the time of her writing) there were more than one million young people—mainly adult males who avoid human contact by shutting themselves in their rooms to indulge in a screen life.

In 2012, there appeared a case of a young Korean male video addict who collapsed and died after a forty-hour session of video games.

> No man is an island,
> Entire of itself,
> Every man is a piece of the continent,
> A part of the main.
> (John Donne—*"Devotions,"* XV11.)

Perhaps Donne is echoing the warning that no single person can function in isolation. We need human interactions.

Lucky are the children whose parents have inculcated in them the love of reading. Parents and teachers have traditionally played an important guiding role here. We have excellent library facilities throughout Australia. The educational programmes in the Art Galleries and libraries in Brisbane are something to be envied, not an insignificant competitor against the electronic marvels of the day. Our children are given all the opportunities to enjoy a more meaningful and richer intellectual life made possible by discount tickets to cultural entertainment.

I have never forgotten the occasion, in the 1980s, when I came upon a young High Schoolgirl in China weighed down by a load of English Literature books—Charles Dickens' *Great Expectations,* Thomas Hardy's *Mayor of Casterbridge,* William Thackeray's *Vanity Fair* and a couple of poetry books. She spoke rather halting and poor English. It was not surprising that the heaviest volume of the pile was an English-Chinese Dictionary. I suspect its life span could be very short. This girl deserved to have a good teacher to kindle the joy of Literature in her.

This century, last century, the aim of education remains the same—an insurance for the future, a means to a more secure and meaningful life. The traditional Chinese world of my parents would be seen as elitist, unashamedly practical and realistic. My parents, as with all parents in their era, would make every sacrifice to enable their offspring to get an adequate education to provide them a fighting chance to jostle for a place in the sun. Lucky are the few who could afford to luxuriate in the world of education merely for the enrichment of the intellect and the pursuit of Truth. There had been many idealistic literati of the traditional past who chose a life of scholarship and communion with nature in lieu of glamorous promotions in Court. This was especially so when the Mandarin refused to serve a corrupt government. One such mandarin was Juan Chi (210-63), philosopher, poet and musician, who, by playing the drunken fool managed to survive when many of his contemporaries did not. He was seldom sober, which served to provide his escape route from the intrigues and corruption of the court that he refused to serve under. He was famous for his eighty-one *Yuang-huai* poems through which he found full expression for his spiritual anguish. This collection of poems has been criticised for obscurity by some commentators. Each of them, however, has an allegorical meaning since it was too dangerous for the poet to comment openly on the political situation of the day.

Poem No: 1 and Poem No: 33 are a sample of the *Twenty-one Poems from the "Yung Huai Shih"*:

Expressing My Thoughts.

Poem 1.
"In the deep of night I found I could not sleep . . .
I paced up and down wondering what I should see . . ."*[5]

What the poet "see" were thoughts that caused him grief to his heavy heart. The backdrop of a breezy moonlit night punctuated by the call of a lonely goose and the cry of a bird hovering over the woods accentuated his melancholy—he felt trapped in the dangerous intrigue of the court.

Commentators in their attempt to put a political slant to the poem allege that the lonely goose symbolises the wise man, disregarded by the rulers of Wei. The crying bird, to me, represents the frustration of the moral Ministers.

Poem No: 33.

"Just one more day and then just one more dusk,
Just one more dusk and then just one more dawn.
My face has lost its youthful constancy,
My vital spirits wasted and drained away . . ."*6

The lines suggest a dreary exhaustion and highlight the poet's mental anguish at the corruption and intrigue of the government of the day. His responsibilities in the service weighed heavily on his heart; he knew that it was too dangerous to express his true feelings. This was the "searing flames" that burnt up his system. He was a prisoner of his own conscience while being acutely aware that his precious lifeblood was ebbing away.

Communist China today has come a long way—it is a far departure from the traditional China of my father's day. In the eyes of a traditional Chinese, the mark of a true scholar was therefore one who had a thorough knowledge of the Confucian Classics and traditional literature. Such scholarship would appear to synonymously elevate him to the status of revered respectability—the educated man would be deemed to be a civilized, wise and moral individual. Thus the humanizing and moral influence of education would be seen to be of paramount importance . . . This respect for scholarship would be reflected in the Chinese habit of referring to "the Sages of Old . . ." especially in times of momentous decisions. The axiom "Education maketh a man" is certainly held dear by the Chinese, as reflected in the following:

The Superior Man—"a person endowed with integrity, intelligence and character. A sage-scholar gentleman all rolled into one."*7

Mencius, one of Confucius' most brilliant disciples had this to say:

". . . esteem virtue and honour virtuous scholars giving the worthiest among them places of dignity, and the able, offices of trust."*8

Strictly speaking, only the Mandarin, the literati class who had passed the stringent Chinese Civil Examinations would wear the scholar label with pride and dignity. Alas! This class of people who had striven to earn this honour at great personal sacrifice and that of their family has become a prehistoric class overnight—with the emergence of a New China at the dawn of the Twentieth Century.

A glance at the definition of the ideal man takes me to:

Greek philosophy:	One who can reason.
Buddhism:	One who excels all other beings in terms of mind and its development.
Chinese philosophy:	Man means *"human heartedness"*.
Indian philosophy:	One who has a perfect soul.

CHAPTER 12

DEATH'S ANTECHAMBER

"But at my back I always hear
Time's winged chariot hurrying near."

Father had a way of teaching us about life and ethics through interesting stories. A lesson on codes of conduct, especially that of courage and love of the family took us to the animal kingdom. One story that made an impression on me was about a fight between two tribes of baboons. The fierce conflict took place at the base of a fallen tree trunk which was leaning against the edge of a cliff. This strategic base had to be kept clear as the tree trunk was a busy escape route for the female baboons and their young. The male baboons were fighting to ensure the safety of their tribe.

Father took pains to illustrate to us how the animal kingdom utilized tribal co-operation which stemmed from the need for survival. We humans are credited with altruistic instincts and this thankfully comes to the fore in situations when one is in dire straits. Migrants all over the world very naturally establish their own form of life-line in their ethnic communities. This was especially so in the less crowded world of yesteryear. An active network of assistance and lifelines in the form of benevolent clubs, associations etc. was a common feature.

Among the Chinese migrants into South East Asia, this chain of inter-connecting helpline had devolved into more specific arenas—they served dialect groups, clan groups, or even migrants from specific areas of the home country. Emigrants from China, mainly from Southern China, present-day Guandong Province, radiated into SE Asia at the turn of the Twentieth Century. We therefore saw the emergence of the different dialect groups such as the Cantonese, Hokkien or Hakka forming their respective associations and societies. Being a Teochew, father became a very active committee member in the Teochew and "Lee" benevolent societies till blindness overcame him. Memorial plaques with portraits of active members of associations and societies decked the hall of the Ceremonial Temple at the entrance to the Chinese Cemetery where father was buried. We were proud to note his smiling face among the rows of past members. All these beautiful portraits were grouped in the year of service which gave an interesting study of historical changes in attire through the century dating right back to pig-tail gentlemen in Manchu attire.

Clan Associations or *"kongsis"* in British Malaya and throughout S.E. Asia were of two kinds: there were the family associations with their ancestral temples and clan associations for those who came from the same village or district in China even though they did not share the same surnames. Villages with the common surnames in Southern China had been known to exist. However, a Chinese, especially in the halcyon days of emigration would find affinity automatically simply because they were "kinsmen" from the same country. It was very common for Chinese to find solidarity with people of the same surnames even though they spoke different dialects and came from totally different prefectures in their home country.

These clan associations and societies in the Malaya and Singapore that I knew of would be the life-line of newcomers—these places would be their first port-of-call. With no knowledge of English and the local dialect, with no hope of any official government employment, they would depend very heavily on clan and benevolent societies which survived on public donations and volunteers. The help-line stretched from providing food, shelter and employment to help unto death to some. Stories abound of Chinese philanthropists who gave millions of dollars to help their kinsmen from the Old Country, All Chinese schools, colleges and universities survived, thanks to the charity of such philanthropists whose kinsmen in turn, paid their homage with the proud erection of statues and plaques not only in their adopted countries but back home in China. These people were father's role models, and in serving these benevolent institutions, he became part of this wide fraternity which served Singapore and Malaya. Father too, had often been feted and he in turn, reciprocated with invitations to home dinners as lavishly and as often as he could.

The Chinese were immensely proud of the many "rag-to-riches" philanthropists without whose selfless giving, thousands of Chinese migrants might have had difficulty surviving. An entire clan would celebrate a clansman's success as proudly as that of their own flesh and blood. The reputations of many of these philanthropists have gone down in history. Father believed that tradition and culture must be kept alive through the observation of rites and ceremonies. It was, and still is, especially in the non-Westernised Chinese communities, the practice to attach great importance to at least three important occasions in one's life—times of birth, marriage and death. These occasions involve the attendance and support of the entire extended family that often spread beyond relatives and even members of the same clan. The length of the period of observation depends on how wealthy or important the family is. The host family is expected to provide lavish dinners to all the well-wishers who, in turn, would contribute cash in envelopes by way of present— red envelopes (ang pows) on happy occasions and white envelopes at a death ceremony.

Wedding and death ceremonies were always a very elaborate affair which could last for a week or even several weeks as in the case of a death in a wealthy family. On such occasions, especially in the case of weddings, many Chinese families have been known to fall into the trap of "saving face" at all cost. Even impoverished families have been known to throw away their life saving and even get into life-long debts in order to "save face."

The ceremony for the dead is considered sacred and in my parents' time such a ceremony had been very elaborate and demanding of the family in mourning. Filial piety demanded as long as a three-year mourning period in the death of a parent. The need to revere the dead after death is on-going in the practice of ancestor worship. This would account for why sons in the family are more important than daughters. Naturally it becomes the duty of the son to revere the parents in ancestor worship on important occasions—they have to be remembered on feast days and in particular on the anniversary of their death. Daughters on the other hand, are not obliged to carry out this duty since they do not have the privilege of bearing the family name. When daughters marry, the Chinese would consider them as "married out of the family"—they bear their husbands' names and have to "worship" their husbands' ancestors.

Our parents reflected the Chinese view that it is only at the hour of death that one could sum up how successful, lucky or unlucky one's life had been. It is viewed by the Chinese that one comes howling into this world and the ideal is to depart this world peacefully and happy in the knowledge that one will be mourned and remembered by the family. Thus the observation of funeral rites and ancestor worship has become entrenched as a sacred duty of one's progeny. The worst fate would be the "curse" of a lonely death, unmourned and unremembered.

It became a social responsibility of benevolent institutions to give the unfortunate homeless and derelicts in society a place to die in dignity and be buried with appropriate funeral ceremonies. This gave rise to the existence of "Death Houses" funded by public donations. These became a place where the homeless and derelicts who were terminally ill, literally waited for death and were comforted by the assurance of a proper burial. I remember coming across one of these "Death Antechambers" right in the middle of Chinatown in Kuala Lumpur where

I lived. This particular building was a mere two-storey "terrace shop house" a common feature of a township and city in Malaya and S.E. Asia. It catered for both sexes and was right in the middle of a bustling environ with all the clamour of busy everyday living. The residents, old, hollow-eyed, emaciated shadows of human beings lounged on their stools or hard-back chairs in the building or just outside the building, on the pavement, too inert to worry about passers-by brushing against them.

The Chinese are inclined to be fatalists and these derelicts were no different. Just as they took life for granted, so did they view the prospect of death with philosophical patience. Passers-by simply took them for granted. Perhaps those who could lounge about counted themselves lucky not to be bedridden. They passed the time in desultory conversations with the other inmates, but in the main they were passively immersed in the hustle and bustle of life about them. With no television or radio or in fact any form of social entertainment, one would hope that they were quite happy to have diversion of any kind.

This building was bleak and depressing—amenities seemed to be adequate but very, very basic. The front portion of the shop was divided by a wooden partition which separated the "bedroom" from the other half which was the funeral parlour where ceremonies for the dead were carried out. The inevitable altar presided in the dark recess of the back wall facing the street. The table always had a ceramic statue of the God of Heaven flanked by his two fearsome-looking guards in heavy, antiquated armour. The altar was as rickety as it was dusty. So was the worn-out white ceramic joss-stick urn painted with a languishing blue floral design. The mandatory joss sticks lit up first thing in the morning by the male care-taker would have flickered their last breath by late morning. The ever-present four oranges or mandarins on a plate (symbolising good luck and wealth) with the obligatory three cups of Chinese tea seemed to be as desolate as the tattered inmates. The perpetual odour of stale incense of joss sticks and burnt-out candles accentuated the sobriety of the atmosphere.

Against the wall, adjacent to the wooden partition that separated the bedroom from the funeral parlour, was an oblong table with two hot-water flasks, a pot of Chinese tea on a tray encircled by some eight stained Chinese teacups. There was a small aluminum basin of not-too-clear water for those who cared to remember to dip their chipped and stained cup for a token rinse before use. The only decoration in this vast dreary room seemed to be some old Chinese scrolls behind a stained little table. Naturally, the other two "decorations" were two aluminum spittoons thoughtfully painted with a pink cherry blossom if only to detract the gaze from its indelible smudges and dirt. There were always some old and outdated newspapers about the table which seemed to have weathered the clutch of many hands, and they too seemed to be breathing their last. Any and everything was stained or tattered.

This ground floor dormitory reserved for the terminally ill, featured two rows of two-tiered wooden bunks separated by a passage-way not unlike the arrangement of sleepers in a railway cabin. A straw mat and a limp rag of a worn-out, thin blanket took the place of bed sheets.

There was absolutely no privacy. Some enterprising occupants of the beds would string a piece of cloth or towel horizontally across their bunks to get whatever privacy they could, at the expense of air circulation and light. For the lucky few, their entire worldly possessions were tucked in small cardboard boxes or plastic bags stuffed under the lower bunks and two corners of the dormitory. No item of furniture was possible in this crowded room. On the same horizontal string strung across the bed would be their home decorations in the way of their life possessions—an army aluminum mug and bowl, a spoon or two, a change of clothes, a dry pandan-leaf fan, sometimes a sad misshapen pipe . . .

Two naked light bulbs from the high ceiling above did their best to illuminate the long, dreary room. Unfortunately, the two faint patches of orange light seemed to accentuate the general bleakness, and when the silent figures emerged from the faint circle of light into the shadows, the ghostliness and eeriness of this sad place certainly lived up to its reputation of being death's waiting-room.

The only bathroom and toilet were situated at the back of the ground floor building. The bathroom was a mere cubicle with a concrete floor and a concreted enclosure for water with a scooper for the use of the bather. There was no hot water provided. Hot water taps were unheard of in such a place.

The toilet, as with most toilets in those days for poor quarters, was only for squatting purposes over a mere hole below which was a bucket—a busy meeting-place for blue bottles and flies. By no stretch of the imagination could anyone be prepared for a revolting pulsating luminescence of different shades of blues, greens and browns as the scavengers laboured away at the putrid mound. These buckets were emptied daily by Indian night soil men.

Depressive or neurotic behaviour among these lonely souls seemed to be unheard of. This was a deserved blessing indeed. These zombies seemed to be resigned to their fate that it was their duty to be merely waiting . . . just waiting . . . . or listening . . . .

> But at my back I always hear
> Time's winged chariot hurrying near:
> And yonder all before us lie
> Deserts of vast eternity.
> (Andrew Marvell—*To His Coy Mistress.*)

Each day was taken calmly in its stride. Life seemed to revolve around the three meals: watery rice gruel with some form of preserved vegetables for breakfast. The daily meals—basic, nutrient-poor food—were from public donation. The lucky few would survive on meals brought by their families or clan members.

The resilience and stoicism of the desolate and lonely was most inspiring—most of them looked on the bright side of the situation. The popular mantra seemed to be "never mind, it is our fate—we should be grateful as long as we can get through the day with enough to eat . . . ." The Buddhist belief in reincarnation of a better life in the next rebirth was always a comforting crutch to cling onto. It would be difficult to read the thoughts behind the lifeless, glassy eyes.

Could the thought be that their pain and silent suffering was an illusion? Could that be of any help? Could Prospero's sentiment help?

> ". . . . We are such stuff
> As dreams are made on, and our little life
> Is rounded with a sleep."
> (*The Tempest* Act IV, Scene 1.)

Perhaps being a Taoist might help after all? If these men were so resigned to remaining steadfast in the face of adversity, a section of Lao Tzu's poem Number 33, from *The Way of Life springs* to mind:

> The conqueror of men is powerful;
> The master of himself is strong.
> Endurance is to keep one's place;
> Long life it is to die and not perish.

The Taoist mystic in the person will help him to accept death as he accepts life; he knows his place in nature and the scheme of things. Therefore he does not perish.

I believe the Death House that I came across in Chinatown in Kuala Lumpur was one of a few others existing in various parts of Malaya. Death Houses in Malaya were not congregated in one street such as those in the famous Sago Lane in Singapore. Sharon Teng (in her article on Sago Lane, in Biblioasia—January-March 2013 issue) provides an illuminating picture of Sago Lane in Singapore of the 1920s). Singapore with a more dense Chinese population than Malaya had more Death Houses to cater for the overflow of population in Chinatown. Thus at the turn of the last century, the street was labelled "Street of the Dead" by the Chinese. Sago Lane then was a bustling, thriving environ of Chinatown, with its specialised allied trade establishments, concomitant with the needs generated by the Death Houses and became an invaluable asset to the over populated Chinatown

Prior to World War II, Singapore Chinatown with a spatial extent of two square kilometres had one third of the municipal population—66,000 people, 91% of which were Chinese. By 1930, the resulting squatter settlement resulted in people living in crowded, unhealthy conditions. Poor and low income families were crowded in rented cubicles, averaging two-by-three metres in space, often airless, on a single storey of two-to-four-storey shop houses. Each of these shop houses had only a single shared—toilet on the ground floor with a single wooden bucket which was emptied nightly.

With a big family squashed in a crowded cubicle, it was not only impractical to house a terminally ill person but it became a matter of health for the entire family. The situation was exacerbated by the fact that the working family members had no means of looking after them, the only recourse being the reliance on Benevolence Societies and Philanthropy which subsidised these Death Houses.

Many Chinese in this era, fearful of the "unknown"— Western hospitals and medicines chose to spend their last days in these establishments where they were not given any medical care, but they could at least expect a decent burial. The dying members of the families also nurtured the consolation that they were also doing their families a favour—the Chinese are a superstitious people, they do not welcome a death in their homes, believing that it was unlucky and could result in the premises being haunted. It was also too costly to conduct an exorcism apart from facing the ire of the co-tenants.

Death Houses charged different rates, dependent on the family's income. The standard rate, however, was $150.00 which was often waived to those who could not afford this payment. There was also an admission fee of $10.00 and a $1.00 daily payment for the day-and-night attendants including a fee for the dead to be buried in silken robe. Those too poor to pay for this would have their bodies wrapped in straw mats and buried in basic coffins donated by clan members or temples. Generally the ground floor of the building was reserved for the very poor and terminal cases; the top two floors were for the more wealthy paying members. Coffins ranged in price between $120.00 to $1500.00 (Singapore dollars.)

Kwok Mun was one of the oldest Death Houses which had both male and female wards with wooden bunks set in dormitory style. This establishment occupied two shop houses linked together. The ground floor of one served as the admission room while the other one became the mortuary. There were other cheaper establishments which did not have separate facilities for male and female inmates. The occupants slept on mats donated by the public. Those who could afford to pay would be allocated a corner space which offered some privacy. All meals were provided by family members or from donation, and the food was served on newspapers or banana leaves.

Most residents lived a few days only at these places. In the 1940s, there was an average of six deaths a day in these houses for the dying. Coffins would often be found lining up on the pavement whilst waiting for the lorry to transport them for burial. With no embalmment and with the tropical heat, the stench was a nasty contribution to a serious health problem. With too many bodies to handle, funeral rites were often held for two to three corpses simultaneously with separate Daoist priests engaged by different families chanting over their respective coffins. Each priest studiously engaged in his rhythmic chanting in keeping with the tok-tok-tok beating of a little drum punctuated by the intermittent beating of the gong. Ceremonies generally began at eleven in the morning and the cacophony burst out in real earnest with the screeching of the clarinet, loud braying of the trumpet with the clashing of cymbals and rhythmic thundering of the drum. The scene became even more surreal, amidst the acrid smell of candles, joss sticks and the burning of funerary goods such as paper money, (stacks of them), paper cars, paper maids, and servants etc. to serve the dead on the other side. The billowing smoke and shifting flames often distorted one's view of the spectacle. This, with the pressing crowd of onlookers awash with the loud mourning of family members induced a feeling of suffocation in a world of weird, darting shadows helplessly drowning in the dissonance of sound and noise. The spectacle was often a tourist drawcard; but for the residents of the street, they must have a different attitude—lucky would be the ones who could be immune to all this relentless activity day and night; day in, day out.

A wake at the Death House could last for three, five or seven days AND nights, depending on how well off a family was. These family members who visited the dying daily, literally waiting for their demise, would feel it incumbent upon them, (as all Chinese do), to send off their deceased members with the proper celebration of a wake. Such ceremonial rites are still in practice today— the dearly departed must be well looked after on the other shore—the burning of paper effigies today could include a mobile phone, a set of golf clubs or even an aeroplane. Wealth certainly can contribute to bigger and more spectacular bonfires.

Death Houses in Singapore were banned in 1961. This was driven by safety concerns regarding fires, noise pollution, and, particularly, for health reasons. Today's Sago Lane is a tourist mecca for a very different reason—it boasts of modern shopping complexes, exotic food centres, and residential tower blocks serve a different income group of residents. Only a plaque for the information of the tourists testifies the sad existence of a different scenario of the not-too-distant past.

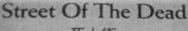

Street Of The Dead
死人街

A funeral parlour, c. 1950
(Courtesy of National Archives of Singapore)

Death houses once lined both sides of Sago Lane. A death house was literally where the poor came to die. Most of Singapore's poor Chinese immigrants lived in overcrowded quarters, where there was hardly enough space for the living, let alone the dying. This, coupled with the superstition that dying in one's home brought bad luck to the remaining residents, led to the creation of death houses. Medical care and facilities at the death house were minimal, for those who entered did not expect to recover. Rooms and dormitories offered the dying a place to rest, while the attached funeral parlours ensured a proper burial.

The dead person would be laid out in a Chinese coffin surrounded by colourful paper effigies of worldly goods, such as money, cars and houses. The effigies would then be burnt with some personal items belonging to the deceased. This ritual symbolised the assurance that wealth and comfort await him in the spirit world.

As dismal as they were, death houses were a vital part of the Chinatown community. They were outlawed in 1961 and shops selling funeral paraphernalia sprung up in their place.

*1 The plaque in today's Chinatown (Singapore).

**2 Sago Lane today

CHAPTER 13

CONFUCIAN DECORUM
VERSUS DAOIST ABANDON

T here are traditionally three belief systems in China—Confucianism, Daoism and Buddhism. These three teachings flow together as naturally as water, enabling a Chinese to blithely claim that he is a Confucianist as well as a Daoist and a Buddhist. The Chinese are not by nature a religious people. Voltaire viewed China as a country without any established church but guided by the teachings of philosophers. The complexity in the make-up of a Chinese can be broadly summed up thus: the intellectuals believe in nothing; the uneducated believe in everything. Popular Daoism and Buddhism recognise a whole pantheon of gods, "immortals", spirits and deities. These omnipresent divinities are there to observe the daily conduct and behaviour of people, which they then report to the presiding judge, the Jade Emperor. It is this omnipotent deity who determines one's future in this world and in the afterlife.

Daoism had been a largely intellectual pursuit until the 2nd century AD, when it was organised as a formal religion and priesthood by a Zhang Daoling, a charismatic pretender who usurped the authority of Lao Zi and claimed to have magical power. Zhang distorted Daoist philosophy and transformed it into a religion with its pantheon of gods and supernaturalism to challenge Buddhism. Buddhism, introduced from India, had flourished especially well in China during the turmoil following the fall of the Han Dynasty.

Confucianism and Daoism can be seen as the "two poles of Chinese tension"—Confucianism deals with rituals, conventions, conformity—in short, it emphasises Man's role in society which entails the subjugation of the individual towards the working of the common good. Daoism, attributed to the teaching of Lao Zi (Lao-tze, 568 BC), on the other hand, focuses on the importance of the individual. It propounds a more romantic, and seeming laxity in attitude towards life. Its keynote is the *"Dao" (Tao)*, loosely translated as the "Way—adhering to the doctrine of *"Wu Wei"*—non-action, non-assertion. Daoism advocates a return to nature—one has to mould one's life in harmony with nature because Man and Society are at the mercy of Mother Nature. Daoism favours the use of intuition and emotion for the benefit of the individual. It perceives Man as part of Nature no different from the flowers, trees and all living things. We are all part of the cycle of birth, decay and death.

Daoism could not become an organized force in Chinese politics: it expressed an alternative to Confucianism in the realm of personal belief but left the field of practical acting to Confucianism. Daoist mystics and poets favoured freedom from time, care and entanglements with bureaucrats and power. They contributed an anarchistic strand and questioned established Confucian organisation which justified the power of the Emperor. A Daoist would not be interested in the encumbrance of duties and responsibilities. "Live and let live" could easily be a Daoist's motto in life. Many a Confucian Mandarin who was unwilling to be involved with court corruptions and intrigues would choose to embrace the solitude of nature to enjoy the Daoist way of life; as naturally and easily as changing one's clothes. Daoism is at variance with Confucius' social semicollectivism, where a person is expected to seek integration into society and to follow the norm. To Confucius, individualism is seen as selfish, one is expected to subjugate one's own interests for the good of society: first, in duty to the family; next, duty to society and then in duty to the country and the world at large. "Doing one's own thing" is, therefore, a social taboo. Social responsibilities are his, for the term of a strict Confucianist's natural life! Daoism represents a rebellion against all this, seeing it as contributing to the artificiality of social life.

A Daoist would be a natural failure in examinations; he would not bother to work towards becoming a Government official. He would prefer his jug of wine. Li Bai, (also known as Li Bo), a brilliant and prolific Daoist poet in the Tang Dynasty comes to mind. He was a consummate drunkard and seemed to perform brilliantly when he was totally besotted. Li Bai was an acclaimed genius and a romantic figure who took traditional poetic form to new heights. Though he never took part in the Civil Service Examination, he was a scholar in his own right and is famous for his thousands of poems which have been much admired through the ages. The Tang Emperor

Xuangzong was so impressed by him that he gave him a post in the prestigious Han Lin Academy to provide scholarly expertise and poetry to the Court.

Li Bai's poems generally celebrate the beauty of nature and solitude, the pleasure of friendship and of course, the joy of drinking wine. His romantic aura gave rise to the legend that he died trying to clasp the reflection of the moon in the river from his boat.

The following poem is one of his gifts to China:

WAKING FROM DRUNKENNESS ON A SPRING DAY.

> "Life in the World is but a big dream;
> I will not spoil it by any labour or care."
> So saying, I was drunk all the day,
> Lying helpless at the porch in front of my door.
> When I woke up, I blinked at the garden-lawn;
> A lonely bird was singing amid the flowers.
> I asked myself, had the day been wet or fine?
> The Spring wind was telling the mango-bird.
> Moved by its song I soon began to sigh,
> And as wine was there I filled my own cup.
> Wildly singing I waited for the moon to rise;
> When my song was over, all my senses had gone. [*1]

"Gone fishing" was another Daoist ploy to withdraw from the encumbrance of life. Fishing, with the contemplation of the changing element of water that it involves was, in fact, an accepted gesture of withdrawal from imperial office. It could, alternatively, be a symbolic gesture for a banished or unemployed official to fish his way into office. History has it that Jiang Taigong, the advisor to the founder of the Zhou Dynasty (1027-256 BC) was well known for fishing his way to official appointment. He was found fishing with no hook attached to the fishing line in the belief that the fish would come to him of its own volition. King Wen of Zhou hired him; he needed a sage to advise him on how to win the empire. His son, King Wu, using Jiang's strategy of waiting for the right moment to go into battle managed to overthrow the Shang Dynasty.

The *Tao Te Ching*, the Bible of Daoists was attributed to Lao Zi (571BC). It is a little book of eighty-one separate cryptic verses with a profundity of thought and subtlety of word arrangement which lends itself to various interpretations. Its central theme, the *"Dao"*, (the Way) embodies the concept of the order of Nature and advocates non-interference: one must allow nature to take its spontaneous course. Time never stops; there is incessant transformation as in the flowing stream where no state can remain static. Change alone is constant. However, as every action brings about a reaction, this retains the eternal balance of the universe, the Cosmos. Life is fragile, and this impermanence, this transiency stretches to human sentiments and relationships as well.

There was a story about Zhuang Zi by an unknown Ming author to illustrate this. Zhuang Zi, after rejecting an offer of a ministerial appointment by the King of Chu decided to live a quiet life and indulge in the peace and beauty of Nature. In the course of his wandering, he happened to stumble upon a cemetery and was intrigued by the sight of a young woman fanning a wet grave furiously. In answer to his query, she informed him that the grave belonged to her loving husband. They had been deeply in love and he had made her promise that she should not remarry as long as his grave remained wet and moist. She was fanning to hasten its drying.

Zhuang Zi, the prominent Daoist philosopher, born 200 years after Lao Zi, (365 BC) assumed the mantle of Daoist master. His book of the same name, *(Zhuang Zi)* developed the concept of the *Tao Te Ching*. He was highly revered and was elevated to the status of "immortal" just as his master, Lao Zi was. Zhuang Zi was known for his famous dream in which he was convinced that he was a carefree butterfly flitting from flower to flower. When he woke up from his sleep, he was in a confused state— he wondered if he did really dream about the butterfly or could it be that he was really the butterfly dreaming about Zhuang Zi?

Daoism propagates spiritual freedom. The non-action philosophy maintains the wisdom of going with the flow of Nature to achieve enlightenment and contentment. Man should accept that the *"Dao"* of everything in the universe lies in the acceptance of the natural cycle of Change—the cycle of birth, death and rebirth because Man is intrinsically part of Nature. When his beloved wife died, he shocked his disciples by singing in time to his beating on an upturned basin by her coffin. His reply to the question of his incredulous disciples was:

> "When she died, I was in despair. But soon, I told myself that in death nothing new has happened. In the beginning, we lacked not only life, but form. Not only form but spirit. We were

blended in one great featureless indistinguishable mass. Then the time arrived when the mass evolved spirit, spirit evolved form and form evolved life.

Now life in turn has evolved death. Besides nature, man's being also has its seasons: his own sequence of spring and autumn, summer and winter. If someone is tired and lies down to rest, we should not pursue him with cries and laments. I have lost my wife she has laid down to sleep in the Great Inner Room. To disturb her with my tears would only demonstrate that I am ignorant of the Laws of Nature. That's why I am no longer mourning."

Zhuang Zi's concept of the primordial state of the universe and life seems to reflect our contemporary physicists'. He mused further about death in this passage:

"How do I know that wanting to be alive is not a great mistake? How do I know that hating to die is not like thinking one has lost one's way, when all the time one is on the path that leads to home? . . .

While a man is dreaming, he does not know that he dreams; nor can he interpret a dream till the dream is done. It is only when he wakes, that he knows it was a dream. Not till the Great Awakening can he know that all this was One Great Dream . . . ."[*2]

While Confucianism concentrated on the peaceful pursuit of culture, Daoism favoured the promotion of martial arts, sword-play and shadow-boxing. This is in line with the teaching of going with the flow of nature—the need to work with nature by dexterity and balance rather than by brute force. Observation of the fighting tactics of birds and panthers led to the characteristic circling movement of sword exercises, taijiquan and shadow-boxing. Circling movements put man in tune with the movement of the stars and the natural cycle of water as it rises in clouds and falls in rain.

Daoists believe that fighting and battles are part of life; and have been responsible for producing military treatises and military strategies to outwit the enemies. Winning a battle by bluff was the type of ploy favoured by Daoist military strategists. *The Romance of the Three Kingdoms* features a story of a general who deceived the enemy into believing that his undefended city contained a huge army by leaving the city gates wide open while he calmly played the lute on the city walls.

Daoism with its sympathetic and organic approach to nature enabled it to contribute to scientific thought. Immortality is not impossible to a Daoist. Daoism has been associated with alchemy and magic in its effort to secure an elixir of life. It therefore has a strong focus on the improvement of health with attention to the balance of the right food in combination with the need for exercise. Detachment from life through retirement to the wilds, allowing oneself to be immersed in nature keeps one attuned to the rhythm of nature (not forgetting that jug of wine), is a Daoist paradise indeed.

Secret societies in China, whose members have relied on Daoist martial arts and shamanistic powers are known to have flourished throughout Chinese history. They are known for their efforts in the fight against Western powers. One famous society known as the Boxers, the "Harmonious Fists" Society played a significant part in the Boxer Rebellion against the Western nations in 1900 which changed the course of history.

One other time when Daoism appears to have been a contributory factor in Chinese politics is mentioned in connection with the celebration of the Autumn Moon Festival during the Yuan (Mongol) Dynasty. Buddhism and Daoism, with their plethora of deities and immortals featuring in colourful myths and legends, have characterised the celebration of the various Chinese festivals. The mid-autumn festival is believed to have existed as early as the Han Dynasty (156BC). The Han Emperor, Wu Di, initiated celebrations to last for three days including "viewing the moon"evenings with lavish banquets at the Toad Terrace. This festival, celebrated on the 15th day of the 8th lunar month, is noted for the festive lantern lights and the prominence of mooncakes which are exchanged as gifts. This is the night when the moon is believed to be at its biggest and brightest in the year; and women pray to the Moon Goddess for a good marriage. Mooncakes, round in shape and decorated with images of goddesses or a rabbit have various sweet fillings of melon seeds, sweetened cassia blossoms, sweetened bean paste, almonds, eggs etc. The roundness of the cakes is not only a celebration of the beauty and brightness of the moon, but also symbolises unity in the family. Both Daoism and Buddhism believe that the Jade Rabbit who lives in the Moon Palace is responsible for making pills of immortality

One historical reference to mooncakes dates from the period when the Mongols overthrew the Song Dynasty, replacing it with the Yuan Dynasty (1279-1368AD.) The Mongol conquerors treated the subjugated Han Chinese with cruelty; the Southern Han Chinese in particular, were openly traded as slaves. Chinese rebellions against the Yuan Dynasty began as early as 1351; but it was not until 1353 that Zhu Yuanshang, who later became the first emperor of the Ming Dynasty in 1368, was successful in defeating the Mongols and reinstating a Chinese Dynasty. His victory over the Mongols in the Chuzhou Prefecture is said to have been achieved with the help of his senior counsellor, a Liu Bowen, who was a scholar and military strategist known as the "Chinese Nostradamus."

Daoism is credited with a more picturesque slant to this historical episode. As is often the case, the line between historical fact and legend can be rather blur at times. The story goes that the Jade Emperor in his rage had afflicted the city with a plague. One of the Daoist immortals felt sorry for the populace of Chuzhou and sent one of his disciples to save the people of the city. He was none other than Liu Bowen. The first thing he did on reaching the city was to inform the people that he had begged the Jade Emperor to forgive and to spare them. He held Daoist rites and prayers in the city for three days and nights. The people were informed that they would be saved on the proviso that each family, on the night of the Moon festival should raise a flag and have bright lanterns lit. He then distributed a mooncake to each family with instructions that each cake contained a slip of paper with a Daoist incantation and that the cake should not be cut open till the midnight hour of the Moon Festival, the 15th of the month. At this hour, they should beat the drums and gongs as loudly as they could. The using of mooncakes for this purpose was facilitated by the fact that Mongolians did not eat mooncakes and the Chinese are a superstitious people.

The populace followed the instruction, and when they cut open the cakes, they found the slips of paper containing the message: "KILL THE DAZU!" (The Tartars; the Mongols.) Everyone dutifully armed himself with knives and instruments of battle to the cacophony of drumbeats. At the same moment, Zhu Yuanshang and his vast army rushed in for the kill. The ill-prepared Mongols who had no idea of the strength of their attackers fled in confusion and terror.

Buddhism and Daoism have brought a breath of fresh air into the sterile rigidity of the Confucian world. Their contribution to the arts has enriched the Chinese world, principally through the delightful legacy of Chinese calligraphy and brush paintings by Confucian scholars. Buddhist and Daoist teachings and beliefs have had a pervasive influence on Chinese political and cultural heritage. Confucian rites, ceremonies and Chinese festivals have a strong Buddhist and Daoist flavour. The Qing Ming Festival, (the grave-cleaning day), a mandatory observance based on the central Confucian tenet of filial piety and ancestor worship has absorbed the inclusion of prayers to Buddhist and Daoist deities.

Father's death was the first in our family and on Qing Ming Festival day it became our turn to kowtow to him the way he had shown us in those bygone days. On that morning when the living gathered to remember the deceased loved ones, we, too, muddled our way through with our mother taking the supervisory role of head of the family. Mother, who had been brought up in a Catholic family had no idea or interest in Confucian rites and ceremonies. It was a case of our following a blind leader.

I used to wonder if our mother had slept the night before, especially when everything was so strange and new to us on our first visit to our father's tomb. We had to be packed ready to leave by four o'clock, before dawn, at the latest, for the simple reason that thousands of other devout Chinese would be making the same pilgrimage. Unfortunately, there was always a fearful bottleneck at one section of the only entry road to the three hills of the cemetery. The serpentine cavalcade of cars, motor cycles, loaded bicycles and heavily loaded pedestrians had one single purpose—to beat the sunrise. The next human queue would be at the entrance temple of the cemetery where all devotees had to ask the presiding deity for permission to enter the cemetery. One and all, with joss-sticks and offerings of sweetmeats, would kowtow with speedy reverence and after planting their joss-sticks in the big urn, would pack away their ritualistic offerings with none-too ceremonious reverence, and rushed hell-bent in the direction of the graves.

The undulating line of worshippers in twos and threes trudging behind swinging torchlight or lanterns engulfed in muffled conversation in the dawning had a binding charm of its own. Some awesome authority seemed to preside in this magic hour between darkness and light; conversations automatically took the form of reverend whispers. The radiating shafts of sunlight spreadeagled across the vast velvety blue sky would wantonly touch the edge of the rising mist. Gently and flirtatiously, a pink gossamer thread of light would shimmer coquettishly before enfolding the hills and valleys in its welcome embrace to the tentative twitter of waking birds.

Very soon, with the benediction of more light, the birds were encouraged to contribute their ode to joy in the celebration of the birth of a new day with a pot-pourri of chirping and cooing and chirruping and fluting . . . . There was always a great sigh of joyous relief when one reached the grave and could, for the first time, spare a moment to appreciate the beauty of dawn which, like a curtain being drawn, revealed a scene of teeming human ants winding all over the hills. The atmosphere of warm camaraderie and single-mindedness of common purpose was electric; each and every one seemed to be rushing through similar chores—shovels and shears rose and fell while blades of cut grass swirled around; the womenfolk would be busy kneeling and scrubbing the graves and headstones. Everyone worked with a will and the soft light of the morning soon displayed the crowded scene of individuals praying with reverence at the family graves. Burning joss sticks and candles heralded the reunion of the living with their departed loved ones. We too, reverently muttered our private messages to Father, without whom we felt quite lost. Courtesy and good will of every individual was manifested in the unsolicited teamwork to clear and tidy any abandoned graves in the immediate vicinity of the family grave. We always put an extra candle and three joss sticks at any abandoned, derelict grave next to Father's.

This was the day when we had to copy what others did. The pang it brought was searingly hot indeed. On this our very first visit to a family cemetery, our first All Souls' Day observance suddenly opened out to me a strange, surreal world of timorous wonder at our having to make an attempt to forge a connection with our dead father who was entombed under the heavy concrete slab. I was certain that we all had difficulty reconciling ourselves to the fact that Father would never ever be living with us again; his empty chair would always remain empty.

This same gripping pain seemed to burn through me some years later when I had to face the passing away of Mother. We lost our mother in 1999. Mother's quiet departure reflected her elegance and self-effacing nature. The night of her burial was dark and stormy and it suddenly occurred to me that she was all alone in a cold, dark grave on a lightning-flashing night. Her loneliness seemed to be all the more poignant to me when I remembered that she had never ventured out alone in her life without the company of at least one member of the family. The only time she did venture out on her own was to visit me when I was living in Tasmania. It was a phenomenal act of determination and courage which bordered on the miraculous when she first came into view at the door of the plane in Launceston.

Our happy life in Australia was all too short. She left me a beautiful garden with her favourite rose shrubs which she had tended with love and care. She had meant to return to spend Christmas with me in 1999, but this time she failed to get back to me. Mother passed away in September.

> Last year today,
> My mother, patient and trusting,
> Gratefully we enjoyed life's offering.
> This time today.

> Whither away?
> The dear face gone—she left behind
> Rose blossoms laughing in the wind.
> Christmas today.
> (Christmas 1999.)

Wordsworth's *Lucy* poem always comes to mind whenever I think of my mother.

> A violet by a mossy stone
>   Half hidden from the eye!
> Fair as a star, when only one
>   Is shining in the sky.

> She lived unknown, and few could know
>   When Lucy ceased to be:
> But she is in her grave, and oh,
>   The difference to me.

I muttered to Father as I did years later to my mother that I would always remember them in my waking hours— their memory would always be with me simply because Nature is eternal. I am inclined to take comfort in the belief that our loved ones will be as real to us as long as Nature exists. Surely the loved departed souls must have dissolved and become one in the beauty of Nature—in the hill, in the roaring waterfall, in the clear waters of the spring . . . they too, are with Wordsworth's ". . . Presence that disturbs me with the joy of elevated thought." With apologies to Wordsworth, I'd like to cling to the wishful hope that I see my parents

> "Whose dwelling is the light of setting suns,
> And the round ocean and the living air,
> And the blue sky . . ."

Various religions and teachings express the notion that our body is the temple of God—yes: from dust we came and to dust we shall return—"Ashes to ashes, dust to dust" seems to have a familiar ring of reunion with Mother Nature . . . Daoism is very much alive here. Are the goodbyes at death's door to be that final? Will we not meet again?

CHAPTER 14

AS LONELY AS AN AUTUMN LEAF
UPON A LONELY OCEAN

This is perhaps the most difficult and painful chapter of the book.

It was at about ten o' clock on a Sunday night as my Vespa scooter phut-phutted home after I had dropped my pillion rider off at her home. She was the only other girl in our group which had just returned from a demanding weekend interstate where our Vespa club had a friendly challenge with another club in a gymkhana. The narrow, winding road home in darkness from about 120 miles from home had seemed particularly difficult after that tiring weekend. This was really the first time that I had travelled that far on my scooter.

It was past sleep time for the family when I finally arrived home. I have no recollection of where the rest of the family was. The dining-room presented me with an awful scene: My blind father was standing near mother, who appeared to be clutching at her heart and gasping for breath; she seemed to be teary and in great distress. Father appeared to be shouting angrily at her. He too, was in a state of distress and, being blind, he was not aware of mum's physical situation. All this transpired because his eldest daughter who had been away on her Vespa scooter since Saturday morning had yet to return home. I don't recall if father had been cognizant of the fact that I was to be away from home for the entire weekend. It is possible that I had not asked for his permission to do this fearing that he would object. Father, in his blindness, would often imagine and magnify his fears and worries. It seemed to me that his fury at my mother might stem from a suspicion that she had "conspired" with me and he had no idea why I had not been home during the weekend.

I was quite exhausted, and in an impulsive fit of fury I shouted at father: "Why can't you be a man and take it out on me, the culprit, instead? I hate you!" There was a dead silence. This is my last recollection of the situation before my head hit the pillow. It had been my first priority to get a good night's sleep so as to be fresh for the morning's Inter-School Debate. The entire school and guests were to attend the session and, being the teacher in charge of the debate, I was anxious that nothing should go wrong. I remember that at some time in the night, I did wake up momentarily with a cold fear streaking down my spine and a vague constriction in my throat; but I was immediately drowned in deep sleep again.

The entire family was woken up at dawn by a distraught mother in a state of shock. Mum had gone to the toilet, which was adjacent to the bathroom. Father was right there at the door of the bathroom—he had hanged himself with my Judo belt tied to the lintel. A blackness seemed to descend upon me as I gasped: "Oh God! Father! I dare not come to you. I am frightened . . ." A type of amnesia seemed to seep through my system, which succeeded in blocking out many memories from that chunk of my life. A total blank took over. All I knew was that I seemed to be groping about the house in a blind mist till daybreak.

My cowardly recoil from reaching out to my dead father stems from a phobia of an inexplicable fear of the dead. This deep-seated terror of facing any dead person has had an abiding grip on me all through my life. I have no recollection of who cradled Father and took him from the bathroom—it would have to be my traumatised mother and brother. I seemed to be groping in a surreal mist till about seven in the morning, when I rang up a friend who had the unfortunate greeting of the day: "My father has hanged himself." Still in a slow-dance motion, I got dressed to go to school. The Principal of the school (a Catholic nun) was on the stage in the assembly hall checking the set-up for the great debate. I wished her "good morning" in the most natural manner and said in the coldest of fashion: "Sister, I am afraid I can't come to school today. My father has hanged himself." Perhaps Sister was too absorbed in what she was doing; she just asked me to help her to shift a table. I did so automatically and nonchalantly repeated my message again.

Back home, the misty curtain enveloped me again. It was as though I was enmeshed in a deep REM sleep and had difficulty opening my eyes. When I did manage to "open my eyes", the sitting-room was cleared of all furniture. It appeared to have become much more spacious—someone had knocked out the wooden barrier that was the wall of Father's room. The one prominent feature in the otherwise empty sitting-room was a fearful-looking Chinese wooden coffin, which had been part of the root of my childhood terror. Chinese funeral rites had been a regular feature of my young days; they were often carried on throughout the night by one family or another. They had been responsible for many nightmares which still trouble me even today. The nightmares were all the more surreal in their very silence—I would often be the only person walking down a deserted street at night and stumbling upon the scene. The big, formidable, solid wooden coffin with numerous white candles and the eternal suffocating lead scent of the burning joss sticks curling and curling into a blinding smoke pall seemed to be stretching out skeletal fingers to ensnare me. Added to this were the numerous frangipani wreaths which exuded a sickly sweet stench of death. The fragrance of frangipani still sends shivers down my spine today. This scene in my horrifying nightmares would feature ghostly sack-cloth shrouded figures circling and circling silently round and round the coffin casting enlarged ghostly shadows which rivalled the misshapen dancing shadows of the white lanterns swinging menacingly in the breeze. Often, in the dead of night, the muffled chanting of monks, with the drums, bells and cymbals of a funeral ceremony would terrify me. I would be fighting against sleep for fear the nightmare might occur again.

The wake following the death of my father lasted three days. I had no idea how and by whom all the funeral arrangements had been made. I was not even aware that our two uncles, Father's brothers, had been among the mourners till I saw the photos later. They had come from another state, Penang, and would not have had any other contacts in our city. The organiser of the entire funeral ceremony and burial (down to the choice of the grave site and the wording on the headstone) may have been some of father's friends and members of the Teo Chew Benevolent Association, of which he had been a long-serving committee member. Father also had many loyal old friends. I had no idea either, of how relatives and friends were informed of the family tragedy.

There were two earlier occasions when I seemed to have broken out of the REM sleep. The first one was my clash with a pompous police inspector accompanied by his assistant police constable. I had no idea where my father was that morning and how he was taken to the hospital mortuary. All I remember is an outburst from my stupor. I seemed to have been in an uncontrolled fit of temper, shouting at the inspector: "GET OUT! GET OUT OF MY HOUSE! My father has just died tragically. How DARE you utter such stupid rubbish?" I remember lurching forward to push him out of the house. The callous man had held out my brown judo belt and accused me of murdering my father on two counts: 1. The judo belt belonged to me. 2. The knot around father's neck was too tidily executed. The inspector did not believe that my father could have done it himself.

After a couple of blank frames in this on-going slide show, at the next awakening from my somnolence, I found myself sitting alone beside an open drain outside the morgue at the public hospital. I don't remember how I got there and how long I had been sitting there. All I can remember is this litany addressed to the blood flowing in the drain: "This is my blood; this is my father's blood . . ."

I had difficulty fighting against the impending "black-outs." My father had been the light of my life and I was physically experiencing the darkness of a closed room with the light switched off. This was a cruel punishment. Being the eldest in the family, I was accustomed to being responsible for the family; yet this eldest, responsible daughter had no idea who had taken charge of the entire funeral ceremony. I did not think that my mother could have risen to the occasion because she too, seemed to be sleep-walking as well. Everything was just so strange and foreign to us. Father's was the first death in the family and under the traumatic circumstances, it was a wonder that my mother was able to hold out till everything was over. Soon after the first one-hundred-day mourning period, she was taken seriously ill and had to be admitted to hospital. My Catholic mother told me that Father had appeared by her bedside in the hospital and told her not to worry, that he would take care of her. The diagnosis was: her illness was "psychological". She appeared to be very ill for some time and we had no idea how she managed to overcome the trauma and resume responsibility as head of the family again.

It must have been at least six weeks after the funeral before I realised that friends, strangers and relatives had flocked in to pay their last respects to father. The Daoist monks' payment had been taken care of as were all other expenses. None of our family members had any inkling about the finances involved.

The funeral ceremony was a demanding chore. Everything had to be done just right—all rituals and observances down to the ranking of sitting and standing arrangement of mourners had to be strictly adhered to. All this naturally was beyond our comprehension. Indeed, we did live up to Father's perception of us: we were "barbarians." During the minimum three successive day-and-night mourning by the family, the coffin remained open and the deceased lay in state. The deceased had to be completely dressed down to the shoes. What he needed in life had to be in the coffin. In my father's case, the most essential item was his walking stick. The deceased's head had to face "inwards"—towards the interior of the house—while his feet had to point towards the exit. This was to facilitate his access to the other world. All statues of deities in the house had to be covered with a red cloth; any mirror had to be removed because seeing any reflection of the coffin in the mirror by anyone would mean ill fortune. A piece of white cloth was hung prominently from the lintel of the front door. White lanterns were lit up at night. All wreaths would be laid about the house, especially around the coffin, with the best and biggest leaning against the front of the coffin. The place of honour for the best and nicest wreath was ironically assigned to the one from the Vespa Club. Many scrolls of cloth inscribed with elegiac couplets appeared mysteriously to lead the funeral procession.

Visitors called in day and night; they came with cash in white envelopes as a form of gift to help to defray funeral expenses. All visitors who came to mourn were presented with three joss sticks and white candles which they would light up when they kow-towed or knelt in front of the coffin. All visitors were also presented with a fan and a white towel to cool themselves, should they wish to accompany the hearse for the burial. Refreshments were served day and night by the family. In some families, visitors who choose to keep the wake in the night often used to play mah-jong or card games to keep themselves awake. This was necessary since the corpse had to be "guarded" and should not be left alone. This would never happen because the monks had to chant and pray every two hours day and night throughout the three days of mourning and the children of the deceased were expected to be on their knees in front of the coffin whenever prayers were chanted. I assuaged my conscience by forcing myself to look at Father when we had to circle round the coffin. To my immense delight and relief, Father in his clean, crisp attire looked truly handsome as if in a peaceful sleep. Father certainly had answered my uncalled-for cowardly prayers that I should be spared being frightened when I looked at him. I had also treacherously prayed that I should be spared being terrified when dreaming about him. In fact, I had shamelessly asked Father not to let me dream about him at all.

It was very much later in the following weeks that I realised that our own daily family meals had been prepared by some unknown person. The clothes had been hand washed by a teaching colleague of mine. Even "Puppy", Father's loyal friend and fierce guardian, which would bare its fangs at strangers and bark at all visitors, had mourned quietly in his own corner and never uttered a sound when he was left unfed. It had been some time before someone remembered to feed the quiet bundle of fur crumped at the far end corner of the house.

My mother who had full control of her emotions at all times might not even have realised that some involuntary stream of tears had coursed down her serene face, especially during the moment before the coffin lid was nailed on. I, who had been sleep-walking for the first two days of the wake, suddenly lost my self-control during this moment. I was not aware that I had collapsed in front of the coffin and was wailing beyond control with the incoherent outburst: "Father! Father! Why do you have to die now when we are out of financial worries?" The dam had burst open; I was not aware of what was happening till someone attempted to lift me from the floor. I had certainly made up for the need to hire a professional wailer. Loud wailing and crying from the mourning family was mandatory. Often, the poor daughter-in-law of the family would have to perform at her dramatic best. There were anecdotes about how some mourners in the family had to be pinched to cry out aloud. Some families had to employ professional wailers to fill the need.

My shocking loss of self-control came about when I saw something which Father had told me about before. Father mentioned that the only functioning faculty left to a deceased person was the sense of hearing and that this was the reason why family members were expected to wail loudly to proclaim their grief to the departed one. Father had also told me that the deceased's method of showing his grief was that "he would bleed from the five orifices." I have forgotten which the five openings were. This was what I saw: blood was bubbling out of Father's mouth and nose. This was beyond comprehension—Father had been a victim of the morgue, he had been dead for three days! I remember crying out in great excitement to the School Principal, the nun who was standing beside me: "Did you see that? Did you see that, Sister?" Her abrupt right about turn to exit the house was another surprise to me.

This drama occurred when the monk summoned the entire family to look at Father for the last time. We were all gathered round the coffin, when the monk broke a comb in two. One half of the comb was supposed to belong to my mother and he threw it out on the street. The other half, purported to belong to Father, was thrown into the coffin. The monk then proclaimed that the bond between Father and his wife was broken; that it was time for Father to be on his way to the other world. The coffin lid snapped to an abrupt close. The next thing I heard was someone calling my name and trying to lift me from the floor.

It was years later before I had the courage to bring up the subject with my mother—no! She had seen nothing! I don't believe that I am a superstitious person; but I have often wondered why I sank to the floor again—was it from the shock belief that Father was trying to let me know that he was sad to leave us? I also wonder if it was all a delusion of an overheated brain.

After a final farewell offering of food and burning of paper money before the coffin was lifted into the hearse, the procession began It was a long procession which stretched from one end of our street to the other. About one hundred and fifty of my students were let off school to accompany Father to the Cemetery. Leading the procession were the bearers of the cloth banners with elegiac sayings or verses followed by the band of Chinese musicians with their pipes, flutes, drums and cymbals. The repertoire of such a traditional Chinese band would generally be some popular Chinese mournful music which was unfamiliar to me. On this day, to my utter surprise and shock, the first piece they played was the Christian hymn "Nearer my God to thee," which would often pull at my heart strings at the best of times. Caught by surprise, I was glad to be able to hide my embarrassing sorrow on the railing of the hearse where the mourners were expected to be. The eldest son, the principal mourner, was expected to carry a long burning joss stick or a bamboo contraption signifying the spirit of the deceased. The children and grandchildren of the deceased were expected to follow the hearse barefooted. We were allowed to wear white socks—the distance to the cemetery was about four miles. The procession had to wind through the main street of the city as a last goodbye trip to the deceased.

Relatives and friends, including the wife of the deceased were excused from walking—cars and buses were available for them. At the freshly dug grave, there was more food, drink and burning of paper money or gifts of paper cars, paper servants or any other earthly conveniences for use in the other world. These were burnt after the coffin had been laid to rest. Father's grave site was fortunately on fairly high ground, on the side of a hill. Feng shui always favours high ground. All sackcloths and cowls worn by the mourners had to be burnt—it was considered bad luck to wear them home.

The first forty-nine days after the burial were considered of great importance. I believe that we had to offer food and pray to our father at the altar at home. Certain prayers had to be said and of course, we had no idea what to do and failed to follow the observances strictly. One observance we had been told was mandatory was on the seventh day after death. It was on the seventh night that the "ghost"—the spirit of the dead person was meant to visit his home to bid a final farewell to his family. All family members were advised to keep to their rooms that night. This we did—we were too frightened to do otherwise and were delighted that one of our relatives, an old lady who knew something about what to do had consented to keep us company that night. She certainly gave us moral courage. We had to offer food and drink to Father at his altar that night. We were aware of anecdotes of families sprinkling talcum powder on the floor to check for any sign or marking of a visit by the dead person. Stories had it that some signs left by the spirit included grains of rice or disarrangement of chopsticks on the altar. It goes without saying that on the night in question; the family were so terrified that we all huddled into my room for the night. The brave lady calmly offered to sleep in the spare room by herself. I was blessedly drugged in a deep sleep right through to morning.

The next morning we discovered two puzzles. First, one of my sisters innocently asked the old lady if she had had a comfortable night or had the night been too warm for her, because my sister had heard her fanning herself in the family dining-room which was just outside my bedroom. This was the location of the chair on which father used to sit at night to fan himself; the scraping of the leaf fan against his clothes was a familiar sound to us. The old lady's answer was an innocent "no."

The next puzzling discovery was by our mother, who chose not to reveal it to us till much later. She had been terrified enough and did not want to sow any more seed of superstitious fear into her children. Mother had noticed, first thing the next morning, that all our wooden clogs had been arranged in a neat row in the family dining-room, a scene we were familiar with. Wooden clogs, quite similar to Dutch clogs, were commonly worn for going to the wet areas of the house, which included the family dining-room, the toilet, bathroom and kitchen. Father, who suffered from insomnia, would resort to the occupation of arranging the family clogs in a neat row at night to pass the time. It had also been his habit to make the nocturnal round of our beds to cover us with the sheet when the weather was cold. I disloyally shivered with cowardly relief that we had been lucky to be in a deep sleep through the night.

I have always regarded with disdain "cheap superstitions" of this sort, but the events of the night did make me wonder and I believe that I have been more cowardly than before. With a view to writing this book, I chose to bring up the subject of these occurrences with my siblings when I visited Malaysia in 2011. No, I had not been dreaming—this had actually happened. Another matter I felt a need to clarify had to do with my eldest brother's dream. This occurred on the evening after our return from the cemetery. Still nervous about a death in the house, my brother managed to persuade some of his friends to stay with us for as long as they could afford. I remember that while the group was playing mah-jong in the living-room, my brother suddenly felt the need to take a siesta. This he did, but it was very soon that a pale-faced brother rushed out of the room to rejoin his friends. What I understand was that during the brief siesta, he dreamt that Father came to him and tweaked his ear saying: "You are the eldest son; you have to take care of the family. Remember?" My brother confirmed that that was what had happened in the dream and that he woke up with a shock. He did not associate the occasion with the mah-jong game, however.

Poor Father! The responsibility of the man of the family was so firmly embedded in him that he was too impatient to wait for the "official" seventh night of the funeral ceremony when the spirit of the deceased was believed to pay its last visit to its home. Father had always taken great pride in being the provider and protector of his families. The little girl had enjoyed many romantic trips with him into the world of romance, myths and stories about the valour and sacrifices of men in protecting and providing for their families. His blindness had deprived him of this important role, prompting this message to his eldest daughter: "I love you. I have to apologise that the Chinese tradition of demeaning and devaluing the female sex is wrong . . ." My unfortunate outburst on the night of his demise certainly signed his death certificate—it would appear that it was time for him to pass on.

His lonely death in the dead of night reinforced the despair and sorrow of his past remark: "I am as lonely as an autumn leaf upon a lonely ocean." There is no point wishing for the Ifs in life—If only I had had the sensitivity to ring up during the weekend to reassure the family that all was well and that I would soon be home safely . . . If only we children had not been so engrossed in our own lives as to whizz past the bowed figure on the chair day in and day out . . . if the eldest child of the family had had the nous to realise that we should give our father more attention. I am truly grateful to Puppy; he must have sensed Father's loneliness when he would crouch by

272 *Jennifer Lee Robertson*

Father's feet and rub his head against them. Father had enjoyed that companionship and told us so.

Father had been an active man, recognised for his contribution to society and in constant demand by friends and relatives. He used to complain that his life was so full that the only time he could get some form of rest was when he was answering the call of nature. His long, dreary world of darkness reinforced the feeling that he was a "Discard" in society and life was meaningless.

This verse comes to mind:

> Into this Universe, and why not knowing,
> Nor *whence*, like Water willy-nilly flowing:
> And out of it, as Wind along the Waste,
> I know not *whither*, willy-nilly blowing.
> (*The Rubaiyat of Omar Khayyam*)

We observed the traditional requirement to mourn for three years. It was not permissible to have a haircut for the first seven weeks of mourning. We children had to wear only black for the first year, blue for the second and a mixture of sombre colours of blue/green and brown was allowed during the third year. We had not been aware that the first 100 days of mourning were crucial—the family would need to offer food and pray to our Father within this period. It seems strange that I have to recount these strange experiences with our dead father as factual.

During one of these periods, on either the 49th or the 100th day of the mourning period, I had a strange experience. I had a dream, and that was perhaps the first and last vivid dream I had of Father in my life. Father was there, in his usual attire but without his walking stick! (Perhaps they had forgotten to put it in his coffin.) What struck me was the expression on his face. It was one of the saddest faces I have seen in my entire life. Father seemed to be shimmering behind a river of flame which separated us and he said to me: "They have beaten me! They have beaten me!" The wretchedness of his expression and message caused me to sit up abruptly in bed. It was quite a miracle to me that I was not in the least frightened. A piercing sadness deprived me of further sleep and I decided to find out from someone what this was all about. The person I went to first thing in the morning was the school tuckshop proprietor who was familiar with matters of this type. She asked me abruptly how long it had been since Father's demise. What she said next really shook me. She asked if we had made our final offerings to Father, to which I answered in the negative. She exclaimed with alarm: "Oh dear me! You have to offer food and wine because yesterday was the day that he had to enter the . . . realm." The term she used was unfamiliar to me. It refers to somewhere in the Underworld, a realm guarded by demons. These demons had to be placated with offerings which Father had not received and that was the reason why they had beaten him! Naturally, our family hurried to make the required offerings that very day.

I must admit that I had previously regarded all this as superstitious nonsense; but the fact remains that the figure of my distressed father was very clear in my mind. It seems to be engraved in my soul. I was deeply shaken and perplexed when other sources confirmed the story, but I chose to remain in a state of sceptical perplexity. My curiosity was heightened, however, when I came across something similar in the Egyptian Book of the Dead— an ancient Egyptian funerary text from as early as 1550 BC. The account resembled the Chinese belief that the deceased was expected to pass through various gates when entering the realm of the Netherworld. These gates were guarded by similar types of vicious demons armed with sharp knives and spears with which they inflicted pain on the deceased if they had not been placated by prayers and offerings of food and wine. Avoiding this ordeal was only made possible through the offerings by the family of the deceased. These demons were grotesque human-like figures with animal heads or a combination of ferocious creatures. They were the same type of figurines that featured in the Haw Par Tiger Balm Garden, the tourist attraction in the 1960s in Singapore.

Since we human beings have a natural sense of retribution, this Tiger Balm Garden with its grotesque display of at least 1000 figurines, depicting all manner of blood-curdling torture to the wicked in the ten courts of Hell could be a comfort balm to those who cry for Justice. Some would like to believe that the ilk of Hitler, Stalin and other blood-thirsty mass-murderers etc., are given their due treatment here. There is a chamber where the sinner is frizzled and fried in a cauldron of boiling oil; other exciting treatments involve being tied to a hot copper pillar and slowly BBQd to death . . . .

Confucius was wise to dismiss speculation of the After-life with a peremptory remark that there is much to engage our concern in this life.

*1 The Mourning

*2 Farewell to Father before his final departure from home

*3 Last family photo with father

*4 The Procession

*5 The Hearse

*[6] Father's final journey through the city.

What a strange and unsavoury dimension I had been thrust into! I certainly prefer to stay in my comfort zone where no demons or devils thrive. I prefer to relive, as I often do, the happiness of the time when Father held me by the hand as we walked along a moonlit path. I may have been about five or six years old when we were meandering leisurely homewards through the woods. Father's strong, warm grasp gave me security and comfort as always. Dusk had fast descended upon us, and when we turned a bend in the path, we were greeted by the pleasant view of a bright, orange glow which lit up the skyline above a hillock. Our gaze was soon rewarded by the appearance of a round, glowing moon climbing steadily over the brow of the hill. There was a whisper of a breeze and as the orange-red pumpkin of a moon rose slowly to her full glory, Time seemed to be stunned into a momentary stillness—the magic of the moment held us in thrall.

Soon the moon was peeping flirtatiously between the branches of the trees, and the dark shadows of gentle dancing leaves created a throbbing mosaic of light and shadow on the forest floor. A subdued sound of running water beckoned us to a nearby river which beamed bright and compelling, as the silver moonbeams twisted their serpentine way to the bottom of the shimmering water— giving the image of an impressive candelabrum dripping dancing diamonds into its depth. The chorus of muted buzzing and clicking of cicadas, amplified by a multitude of sleepy insect murmurs became a timid hum punctuated by the muffled chop, chop, chop of an enthralled nightjar. The muted bird symphony was a tribute to the splendour of the night.

Father who had inculcated in me a love of nature and poetry, pointed to the bright moon and said: "See? She is smiling at us. When we walk towards her, she recedes; you will never catch up with her. She is here, happy to light up our path and give us beauty. If you look carefully, you will see the figure of an old man sitting under a cassia tree." I did try screwing my face for quite a while, and believed that there was some semblance of an old man by a tree. Father is with me all the time, especially on bright moonlight nights. I am still in the habit of looking at the moon and saying: "Father, are you there?"

This was the demon-free world that Father had introduced me to. The six-year-old girl with the page-boy haircut looked up at her father and the surge of love and trust in him on that magical night had its special poignancy. Her father, to her then, was the very essence of poetic beauty and purity. When I look up at the full moon these days, I nurse the belief that he is there, in the Moon Palace, waiting to show me more magical beauty in the world that he now inhabits.

*7 The Moon.

NOTES

Credit is hereby given to scholars' works which have helped towards the writing of this book.

*Bamboo image of cover of book from: Fritz Van Biessen, *The Way of the Brush, Painting Technique of China and Japan,* pub. Rutland, Vermont: Tuttle and Company, Japan, 1962.

Chpt. 1. That Was Then, This Is Now.

*1 Raymond Dawson, *The Chinese Experience,*
   Phoenix Press, pub. 2005, pg 249

Chpt. 2. "Anointed With Fragrance, She Takes Lotus Steps."

*1 The four-inch lily. Photo courtesy of Mona Lim
*2 Shoe of a well-to-do lady. From copy-right-free Wikipedia
*3 Alasdair Clayre, *The Heart of the Dragon,* pub. Collins/Harvill. 1984 page 72
*4 *The Heart of the Dragon . . . ibid page 72.*
*5 *The Heart of the Dragon . . . ibid page 83.*

Chpt. 4. In Walked Father.

*1 *The Wisdom of Confucius,* pub. The Peter Pauper Press, Mt. Vernon, New York, 1963, pg 55

*2 The little girl with the page-boy haircut with her Mum, siblings, servant and maid

Chpt. 5. "There Comes A Time In Our Lives . . ."

*1 Scholar and Cliffs Behind Clouds—Landscape by Ma Yuan,—Fritz Van Briessen, *The Way of the Brush—Painting Techniques of China and Japan,* Pub. Charles E. Tuttle Coy. 1962, pg. 230

*2 Stunning costumes and headgear

*3 Man threatened with sword,

*4 Postures and gesticulations are important in operas.
All photos courtesy of Ray Robertson.

*5 A.De Riencourt, *The Soul of China,* pub. Jonathan Cape, 1959; pg. 132.

Chpt. 6. The Scholar Mandarins.

*1 Raymond Dawson, *The Chinese Experience,* pub.
Phoenix Press of Australia, 2005, pg.35

*2 David Mahony, *Man & Society_Traditional China,* pub. Methuen of Australia, 1977, pg. 33

*3 Raymond Dawson, *The Chinese Experience,* pub.
Phoenix Press, pg 36

*4 Amaury De Riencourt, *The Soul of China,* Jonathan Cape, London, 1959, pg.256

*5 Reprinted by permission of the publisher from *Chinese Calligraphy* by Chiang Yee, pp 232-213, Cambridge, Mass. Harvard University Press, copyright c 1973 by the President and Fellow of Harvard University College.

*6 Luo Guanzhong—translated by C.H. Brewitt-Taylor *Romance of*

The Three Kingdoms, Volume 1, pub. Charles E. Tuttle Company, Japan, 1959 pg. 485

Chpt. 7. No More "Ah Qs".

*1 W.T.Hanes & S. Sanello, *The Opium Wars—pub.* Robson Books, 2003, pg.234

*2 *The Opium Wars,* ibid. pg. 163-164

*3 Dr. Sun Zhongshan—image from copyright-free Wikipedia.

*4 Cixi, the Empress Dowager from copyright-free Wikipedia.

*5 Liu Wu-Chi, *An introduction to Chinese Literature,* Indiana University Press, 1966, pg.267

*6 *The Opium Wars.* (book detail as *1 above) pg.211.

*7 *The Opium Wars* (book detail as *1 above) pg.29.

*8 *The Opium Wars* (book detail as *1 above) pg. 159

*9 The Carving of China from copyright-free Wikipedia.

*10   Close-up of ports affected by the Opium Wars—Map of China after the Opium Wars.—Patricia B. Ebrey, *Cambridge Illustrated History of China,* Pub. CUP Press, 1996, pg. 241.

*11   Map of China after the Opium Wars.—Patricia B. Ebrey, Cambridge Illustrated History of China, Pub. CUP Press, 1996, pg. 241

*12   (Analects IV.5) D. Mahony *Man and Society Traditional China,* pub. Methuen of Australia, 1977, pg 23.

Chpt. 8. "O My Luve's Like A Red, Red Rose."

*1 *The Penguin Book of Chinese Verse* Translated by Robert Kotewall and Norman I Smith, pub. Penguin Books, 1962, pg 18

*2 P.B. Ebrey, *The Cambridge Illustrated History of China,* CUP 1996, PG 34, "Clever men build Cities . . ."

*3 Liu Wu Chi, *An Introduction to Chinese Literature,* Indiana University Press, pub. 1966, pg 221.

Chpt. 9. The Dishonourable "Thousand Gold."

*1 R.B. Blakney (translator) *"The Way of Life—Lao Tzu,* a Mentor Book from New American Library Ltd. Pub. 1955, pg. 131, Verse 78.

*2 (*Analects*—X111: 6.) David Mahony . . . pg.24

*3 P.B. Ebrey: *The Cambridge University Press,* pg 81

*4 David Mahony, . . . pg 24

*5 John Fairbank (edited) *Chinese Thought and Institutions,* Phoenix edu., U. of Chicago Press, Chicago, 1968, page 236.

*6 T.C.Lai & Y.T. Kwong, *Chinese Poetry,* pub. Swindon Book Company, H.K. 1972, pg. 50.

Chpt. 10. "Does A Rose By Any Name Still Smell As Sweet?"

1 Russel Jones: *Chinese Names* Published by Pelanduk, 1997, page 15.

*2 Henry C. Lu: *Legendary Chinese Healing Herbs;* Pelanduk Publications, 1992, pg. 15

*3 Photo of the Teochew (Chouzhou) Benevolent Association in Kuala Lumpur, where father had served as a committee member. Photo courtesy of Leong Chooi Foong.

Chpt. 11. Education And The Ideal Man.

*1 Susan Greenfield, *The Quest for Meaning in the 21st Century*—pub. Sceptre, 2008, pg 10

*2 *Ibid.* Pg. 253.

*3 Ibid. Pg 253

*4 David Mahony, M*an and society—Traditional China,* pub. Methuen of Australia, 1977, pg 28.

*5 J.D. Frodsham and Ch'eng Hsi—*An Anthology of Chinese*

Verse— pub. Oxford Press 1967, pg 53
*6 Ibid. pg 64 *Musings of a First Chinese Daughter* 285
*7 Amaury De Riencourt, *The Soul of China,* pub. Lowe and Brydone, London, 1988, pg. 29
*8 David Mahony—as *4 above. On pg. 29

Chpt. 12. Death's Antechamber.

*1 The plaque in today's Chinatown (Singapore)
   Photo courtesy of Lillian Toh.
*2 Sago Lane Today
   Photo courtesy of Lillian Toh.

Chpt. 13. Confucian Decorum Versus Daoist Abandon.

*1 A. Waley, from Free Project Gutenberg.
*2 Adeline Y. Mah; *Watching the Tree to Catch a Hare,* pub. Harper Collins 2001, pgs. 38-39

Chpt. 14. As Lonely As An Autumn Leaf....

1 The Mourning
*2 Farewell to Father before his final departure from home.
*3 Last family photo with father
*4 The Procession
*5 The Hearse
*6 Father's final journey through the city.
   (family photos)
*7 The Moon.
   (courtesy of Ray Robertson.)

NOTE ON ROMANISATION AND CHINESE CHARACTERS

The pinyin system of Romanization as introduced by Beijing in the 1950s is used widely in this book. Where an older Romanization is likely to be more familiar to read, (eg. Tao Te Ching instead of the pinyin Daodejing), the familiar form is retained.

Traditional Chinese characters rather than the simplified versions are used throughout the book.

NOTE ON SPELLING.

English spelling rather than American spelling is used throughout the book.

BiBLiOGRAPHY AND REFERENCE

I owe an intellectual debt to many of the scholarly works in this reading and reference list.

Adeline Yen Mah, *Watching the Teee to Catch a Hare,* pub. Harper Collins, 2001

Alan W. Watts, *The Way of Zen,* pub. Pelican, 1957.

Alain Peyrefitte, *The Collision of China (British Expedition to China 1792-4),* pub. Harper Collins, 1989

Alasdair Clayre, *The Heart of the Dragon,* pub. Collins/ Harvill, 1984

Amonry De Riencourt, *The Soul of China,* pub. Jonathan Cape, 1959.

Arthur F. Wright, *Confucianism And Chinese Civilization,* pub. Athenium, New York 1964

Barbara Aria with Russell Eng Guan, *The Spirit of the Chinese Character,* pub. Fair Winds Press, 1992

C. Jones, *Through a Glass Darkly—A Journey of Love and Grief with my Father,* ABC books, pub. 2009

C.P. Fitzgerald, *China—A Short Cultural History,* 3rd edition, pub.The Crescent Press, 1961

C. Kinvig, *River Kwai RAILWAY—The History of the Burma-Siam Railroad, Pub. Conway, 2005*

Cao Xueqin, *The Dream of The Red Chamber,* translated by H Bencraft Joly, pub. Tuttle Publishing, 2010

Carol Kendall & Yao-Wen Li, *Sweet and Sour Tales from China,* (Clarion Books) pub. The Bodley Head Ltd; G. Britain, 1978

Ch'u Chai & Winberg Chai (edited and translated) *Essential Works of Confucianism,* pub.Bantam Books London, 1965

Chiang Yee, *Chinese Calligraphy, published* Harvard Paperback, HUP. 1973

Chinese Paintings of the Ming and Qing Dynasties 14th-20th Centuries, printed by Wilke & Coy. Ltd., sponsored by BHP, the Big Australia.

David Mahony, *Man and Society—Traditional China,* pub. Methuen of Australia, 1977

Dong Chensheng, *Paintings of Beijing Opera Characters,* pub. Zhaohua Publishing House, Beijing, 1981.

Edward Fitzgerald, *The Rubaiyat of Omar Khayaam*, first edition 1895, Pub, Collins Clear-Type Press

Fritz Van Briessen, *The Way Of the Brush—Painting Techniques of China and Japan*, pub.Charles E. Tuttle Coy., 1962

George M. Beckmann, *The Modernisation of China and Japan*, A Harper International Student Reprint, 1962

Gianni Guadalupi, *China Revealed—The West Encounters the Celestial Empire*, pub. White Star Publishers. 2003

Henry C. Lu, *Legendary Chinese Healing Herbs*, Pelanduk publication, 1992

H. Sheng *Palace of Eternal Youth*, pub. Foreign Language Press, Beijing, 2nd ed. 1980

J.D. Frodsham & Ch'eng Hsi translated & annotated; *The Anthology of Chinese Verse*, pub. Oxford Press 1967.

James R. Ware (translator). *The Sayings of Confucius*, 5th printing, pub Mentor Book, 1960

Jean-Luc Toula-Breysse, *The Paths of Buddhism*, Pub. Cassell & Co. 2001

Jiang Yu Dai edited and translated, *100 Smiles from Traditional China*, pub. Asiapac Books and Educational Aids Pty. Ltd. 1986

John C.H. Wu, *The Four Seasons of T'ang Paintings*, pub. C.E. Tuttle Coy. Japan, 1972.

John Fairbank (edited) *Chinese Thought and Institutions,* Phoenix education U. of Chicago Press, Chicago, 1968.

John Lee, *Will China Fail? (The Limits and Contradictions of Market Socialism)* pub. The Centre for Independent Studies, 2007.

John Makeham, Chief Consultant, *Ancient Civilisation— China,* pub.Thomas and Hudson Ltd.,2008

K.S Latourette, *The Chinese, Their History and Culture,* 7th Print, pub. Collier Macmillan, 1968

K. Sri Dhammananda *Food for the Thinking Mind,* pub. Buddhist Missionary Society Mission, Malaysia, 1999.

Keong Tow Yung, D.C.Lau, (English translation). *Confucius Says,* pub. Federal Publications, 1982

Lee Siow Mong, *Spectrum of Chinese Culture*, 4th printing, pub. Pelanduk 2009.

Li Weijian (translated), Weng Xianliang, (revised), *Selected Poems by Du Fu.* Pub. Sichuan People's Publishing House, 1986

Lin Yutang (Professor) edited, *The Wisdom of China*, pub. Michael Joseph Ltd. 1948

Lin Yutang (Professor) *My Country and My People,* pub. W. Heineman Ltd., first pub. 1936.

Liu Wu-Chi, *An Introduction to Chinese Literature,* Indiana University Press, 1966.

Luo Guanzhong, *Romance of the Three Kingdoms—Vol.1,* Translation by C.H. Brewitt-Taylor, pub. Charles E. Tuttle Company, Japan 1959

Ong Siew Chey, *Tales from China,* published by Ong Siew Chey, Singapore 2010

P. B. Ebrey, *The Cambridge Illustrated History of China,* pub. Cambridge U.P. 1906

Paul Raffalle, *The Weekend Australian, Dec 5/6 2009*

Paula Delso, *Chinese Horoscopes,* Pub. Pan Books Ltd., 1973

Peter Pauper Press, N. York—*The Wisdom of Confucius,* 1963

R.B. Blakney (translation) *The Way of Life, Lao Tzu,* pub. 1955, A Mentor Book

R. Kotewall & Norman L. Smith translated; edited by A.R. Davis, *The Penguin Book of Chinese Verse,* Pub. Penguin,1962

R. Linssen, *Zen—The Wisdom of the East—A New Way of Life.* Pub. Bay Books, 1972

R. Newnham, *About Chinese,* pub. 1971 Pelican

Raymond Dawson, *The Chinese Experience,* Phoenix Press, pub. 2005

Russel Jones, *Chinese Names,* pub. Pelanduk, 1977.

Selected Jokes from Past Chinese Dynasties 1, pub. Sinolingua Beijing. 1991

Sharon Teng, *Sago Lane, Street of the Dead,* article in Bibloasia—Jan-March, 2013, Vol.8 Issue 4

Susan Greenfield, *The Quest for Meaning in the 21ˢᵗ Century,* pub. Sceptre 2008

T. C. Lai, *Tang Yin, poet/painter 1470-1521,* pub.Kelly &Walsh Ltd., 1971

T.C. Lai & Y.T. Kwong *Chinese Poetry* pub. Swindon Book Coy, H.Kong, 1972

W. Theodore de Bary, *Sources of Chinese Tradition,* pub. Columbia U. Press 1960

W. Travis Haines III/F. Sanello, *The Opium Wars,* pub. Robson Books, 2003

Wu Teh Yao, *Roots of Chinese Culture,* Federal Publications, 1980